The Purposes of Education

Stephen K. Bailey

THE PURPOSES
OF
EDUCATION
By
Stephen Bailey

  PHI DELTA KAPPA
Educational Foundation
Bloomington, Indiana

Perspectives in American Education

This book is one of a five-volume set published by Phi Delta Kappa as part of its national bicentennial year program.
The other titles in the set are:

Values in Education, by Max Lerner
Alternatives in Education, by Vernon Smith, Robert Barr, and Daniel Burke
Women in Education, by Patricia C. Sexton
Melting of the Ethnics: Education of the Immigrants, 1880–1914, by Mark Krug

Introduction

The two hundredth anniversary of the American declaration of separation from the government of England has stimulated millions of words of sentiment, analysis, nostalgia, and expectation. Much of this verbal and pictorial outpouring has been a kind of patriotic breast-beating. Most of it has been rhetoric.

Several years ago the leadership of Phi Delta Kappa announced its determination to offer a significant contribution to the bicentennial celebration in a series of authoritative statements about major facets of American education that would deserve the attention of serious scholars in education, serve the needs of neophytes in the profession, and survive as an important permanent contribution to the educational literature.

The Board of Directors and staff of Phi Delta Kappa, the Board of Governors of the Phi Delta Kappa Educational Foundation, and the Project '76 Implementation Committee all made important contributions to the creation of the Bicentennial Activities Program, of which this set of books is only one of seven notable projects. The entire program has been made possible by the loyal contributions of dedicated Kappans who volunteered as Minutemen, Patriots, and Bell Ringers according to the size of their donations and by the support of the Educational Foundation, based on the generous bequest of George Reavis. The purpose of the Foundation, as stated at its inception, is to contribute to a better understanding of the educative process and the relation of education to human welfare. These five volumes should serve that purpose well.

A number of persons should be recognized for their

contributions to the success of this enterprise. The Board of Governors of the Foundation, under the leadership of Gordon Swanson, persevered in the early planning stages to insure that the effort would be made. Other members of the board during this period were Edgar Dale, Bessie Gabbard, Arliss Roaden, Howard Soule, Bill Turney, and Ted Gordon, now deceased.

The Project '76 Implementation Committee, which wrestled successfully with the myriad details of planning, financing, and publicizing the seven activities, included David Clark, Jack Frymier, James Walden, Forbis Jordan, and Ted Gordon.

The Board of Directors of Phi Delta Kappa, 1976 to 1978, include President Bill L. Turney, President-Elect Gerald Leischuck, Vice Presidents William K. Poston, Rex K. Reckewey, and Ray Tobiason and District Representatives Gerald L. Berry, Jerome G. Kopp, James York, Cecil K. Phillips, Don Park, Philip G. Meissner, and Carrel Anderson.

The major contributors to this set of five perspectives of American education are of course the authors. They have found time in busy professional schedules to produce substantial and memorable manuscripts, both scholarly and readable. They have things to say about education that are worth saying, and they have said them well. They have made a genuine contribution to the literature, helping to make a fitting contribution to the celebration of two hundred years of national freedom. More importantly, they have articulated ideas so basic to the maintenance of that freedom that they should be read and heeded as valued guidelines for the years ahead, hopefully at least another two hundred.

—Lowell Rose
Executive Secretary,
Phi Delta Kappa

To the Free Self of my Daughter Lois

Acknowledgments

My indebtedness is legion: patently to Phi Delta Kappa for "Bicentennial" money to assemble intellectual resources and to support bibliographical searches; to faculty teams who graciously agreed to review my outline with me—at Teachers College, Columbia, convened by Lawrence A. Cremin and Harold Noah; at the University of Chicago, convened by Cyril O. Houle; at Harvard University, convened by Paul N. Ylvisaker; and at Syracuse University, convened by David R. Krathwohl.

In addition, a number of individuals have sent me materials or have discussed my outline or drafts with me. Particular thanks must go to David Clark, David R. Fendrick, Chester E. Finn, Jr., Thomas F. Green, Samuel Halperin, Roger W. Heyns, Cyril O. Houle, Frederick N. Hudson, H. Thomas James, Clark Kerr, Michael W. Kirst, Norman Kurland, Olive Mills, David Riesman, Edward J. Sparling, Jr., Martin Trow, Ralph W. Tyler, and to members of the Aspen Seminar on Higher Education chaired by James A. Perkins. For reasons that become clear in early chapters of the essay, I am especially indebted to Erik Erikson for his intellectual inspiration and personal encouragement.

The Center for Advanced Study in the Behavioral Sciences, Stanford, California, gave me invaluable logistical resources and intellectual peace and quiet during a key stage in the development of this work.

Finally, for the careful and extensive research assistance of my wife and daughter, for the patient typing of Marcia Morey, and for the facilitative behaviors and understanding of my colleagues in the American

Council on Education, notably Roger Heyns, I am deeply grateful.

The necessary absolutions are hereby granted. The work as it appears is mine alone.

Stephen K. Bailey

Washington, D.C.

Contents

Preface

This work is a reflection of both concern and hope.

The concern is that a confluence of technological and cultural forces—what Charles Beard once called "secular drifts"—is turning America into a joyless, aimless, cynical, fragmented, and endlessly contentious society.

The hope is that the best in our past and what is emerging as signs of responsible impatience from the young can come together in formulations of human realities and possibilities which will bring purpose, greater equity, and a new sense of community to the human adventure—in this nation and beyond.

This, then, is an essay in normative moral and political speculation, even though its instrumental focus is education. Most of my writings in political science and government over the years have not been theoretically oriented. However, political theory, read under the inspired tutelage of G.D.H. Cole and Sir Alfred Zimmern at Oxford just prior to World War II, was my first intellectual love. I was struck then, as I continue to be struck, by the inseparability of moral, political, and educational thought. From Plato and Aristotle through Augustine, Aquinas, Comenius, Locke, Rousseau, Pestalozzi, and Froebel, to Dewey and Whitehead, speculations about education have been linked to questions of what constitutes the good life and the good society. Definitions of what in fact constitutes the good life or the good society are and always have been culturally contextual. This essay is no exception. It is addressed to Americans who will live out the decades of the proximate future. The only *eternal* verity I know is that human beings search for the good even as they continue to fumble with shifting definitions and with changing manifestations of evil.

The construction of an essay addressed, as this one is, to common themes in the lives of large numbers of human beings is inevitably plagued by tricks of the mind. Perceptions of reality oscillate with mood and focal distance. Sweeping, sometimes dire, generalizations about "the American people" or "the human condition" trip over roots of divergent reality or promise. Overarching views of "the public interest" dissolve into wisps as "the public" is disaggregated into its tribal diversities. Apocalyptic predictions, which bolster the prophetic ego in so many of us, lose their saliency in the perspective of an eternity of Chicken Littles. Opposites seem as plausible today as they did to Dickens: the best of times, the worst of times; homo sapiens is presently doomed, homo sapiens—at least in evolutionary terms—is simply on schedule; America is leading the decline of the West, America is mankind's last, best hope; the distant roar is an avalanche of desolation, the distant roar is the joyful turning of the tide; human beings are a crummy lot, human beings are only slightly lower than the angels. The very eclecticism of our culture subjects the writer to a kaleidoscope of philosophical, religious, and notional prisms that compete to refract his views of reality.

Perversities lurk even in the ecology of composition. Much of this essay was written over summer vacation in the lake region of western Maine—far from the crowds, tensions, and headlines of the city. Inevitably, the anxieties of March were chastened time and again by the lovely indulgences of July.

So the mind floats its options and spins its doubts. It is steadied only because major signs and portents refuse to disappear. Beyond the tricks of the mind and the felicities of summer are dark and looming shapes that seem to move with the inexorability of the seasons. Two hundred years after its founding, the American nation is fretful and fragmented. Cynical about politics, distressed by inflation, bored by work or anguished by its absence, niggled by the strictures and frustrations imposed by bureaucracies and technologies, enervated by the psychic binds and ego struggles of intimacies, fearful of domestic crime and foreign economic entanglements, weary of the stridencies of social justice, large segments of the American population search simultaneously for psychic shelters and for void-filling novelties and diversions. But there is no hiding place, and, as Santayana pointed out decades ago, most novelties and diversions turn out to be a "treadmill of bitter amusements." Boredom is an endemic disease.

Meanwhile, smaller segments of the American society—smaller but still numerous—find themselves living lives of either quiet or noisy desperation: ghetto blacks and Hispanic Americans, First Americans, the rural poor, unemployed youth, aggrieved women, ex-offenders, forgotten old people. Neglect and discrimination have made many of these subcultures either catatonic or violent.

In short, for multitudes of Americans, the "pursuit of happiness" is a hollow, almost mocking phrase. No compelling social or even personal idea or ideal seems capable of filling the psychic void.

This is happening, furthermore, on an earth suffused with interdependencies and threatened by a malevolent combination of multiple resource exploitations, Balkanized power claims, and existential miseries. At least Americans have the privilege of being bored without suffering the ravages of ubiquitous hunger and disease.

If these conditions are real, and I believe them to be, and if they are unhappy and dangerous, and I believe them to be, what instruments are at our disposal to begin the process of turning things around and getting things together? How can the sullenness that befogs so much of human existence—even among the affluent—be dissipated? Are there ideas or ideals that are capable of commanding loyalty? These are the essential concerns that motivate the construction of this essay.

I hope that what I have written will be widely discussed and will result in pluralistic and practical responses—responses beyond those that have already stimulated and informed this essay. For, intellectually, I am a pluralist; temperamentally, an ameliorist and incrementalist. My faith is in education, in persuasion, in diverse and creative responses to commonly perceived needs, and in the political and social institutions and processes that encourage these phenomena. I distrust both violent and Utopian approaches to the achievement of humane ends. It is true that persistent, palpable injustices in this nation have sometimes led me into considerations of revolutionary change. But fear of a poison far deadlier than the shifting, and I believe shrinking, injustices of a free society—the nonantidotal poison of uncontained autocratic power—has stopped me, and continues to stop me, from giving in to the seductivities of revolution and simplistic ideology.

In this essay, my definition of "educational system" includes but goes far beyond our formal schools, colleges, and universities. In fact, one of my hopes is that by reminding readers of the wealth of educative instruments available to society outside the traditional educational establishment, there may be some chance of focusing and amplifying the functions of the latter while extending and enhancing the work of the traditional core. In any case, I choose to run the risk of definitional amplitude rather than donning a definitional vest too tight for conceptual breathing.

Education and learning are related but they are not synonymous. The educational system, formal and informal, is meant to stimulate learning. But an enormous amount of learning takes place through individual reading, observation, peer interaction, and personal trial and error. In much that follows, individual learning might conceivably be a satisfactory surrogate for the developmental tasks of education. Put another way, if the educational system could motivate continuous learning in the form of lifelong self development, much of what follows would be redundant. It is the seeming inability of the existing educational system to discharge this function satisfactorily that mandates the continuing improvement of the nation's educational services.

A final preliminary: I use the word "existential" in its descriptive, not in its philosophical sense. My division of purposes into "basic" and "instrumental" is a device of convenience to dignify the three fundamental educational purposes postulated in the first chapter.

The Bedrock Realities

A cross the United States as it enters its third century as a sovereign nation, vast numbers of people find themselves increasingly perplexed about the purposes of education. Pupils and students question vaguely why they study what they study. Parents wonder what their escalating taxes and tuitions are actually purchasing for their children. Responsible public executives, legislators, and judges, and their staffs, in the various branches and at the various levels of America's complex constitutional system, find themselves plagued with problems of educational cost and equity. They search for both practical and philosophical definitions and justifications of an educational public interest. Chief state school officers, superintendents, building principals, college and university administrators, and their various associations, search for rhetoric to explain what their educational enterprises are all about and in ways that reassure political and philanthropic patrons and provide some internal reassurance that the political and emotional harassments associated with modern educational administration are worth enduring. Scholars and teachers, traumatized by reductions-in-force and budget stringencies, search for ways beyond the stridencies of collective bargaining to convince others of their essentiality. And, reflecting and refracting all of this perplexity, journalists and educational reformers convey a general sense of educational malaise to a larger public.

In the absence of any comprehensive rationale, and sensing vaguely that the problems of education may be nothing more than the shattered mirror of a larger social disintegration, people tend to settle for narrow goals—"the three Rs," "job training"; for traditional rhetoric—"the liberal arts," "useful skills"; or for banalities—"self-fulfillment," "the whole man." An increasing number of concerned citizens, however, are restive with this tired rhetoric. They sense that the troubled epoch this nation has entered calls for a people so effectively educated in both the arts of living and the political skills of a free society as to preclude immature escapes from reality. They sense that education broadly conceived is the most impressive instrument at the nation's disposal for fighting openly what Camus once called "the death instinct in our times"—for achieving the personal and social maturity needed "to secure the blessing of liberty to ourselves and our posterity."

But even as they think these long thoughts, many Americans suffer the doubts articulated more than a century and a half ago by William Wordsworth in his *Prelude:*

How little those formalities, to which
With overweening trust alone we give
The name of Education, have to do
With real feeling and just sense.

Fortunately, education today connotes something far richer and more diverse than the pedantry of the academies of Wordsworth's day. The educational system might be defined as that combination of social institutions and facilities that are presumed to have as major purposes the discovery and inculcation of knowledge and values and the development of human skills and options. Then the resources at the nation's disposal for these purposes are both diverse and substantial: families, libraries, mass media, journals, books, platters, tapes, churches and synagogues, day-care centers, medical clinics, welfare services, research institutes, industries, unions, agricultural and civic associations—these in addition to our schools, colleges, and universities. All such instruments can and often do function as organic parts of the contemporary educational system.

But what charge is to be laid upon this loose and diverse congeries? To right all wrongs? To agree upon a single holy grail? To "de-school" the society? To prepare people for the shocks of an unknowable future?

The charge must, I believe, be related to a fundamental examination of the bedrock biological and cultural realities of human life in late twentieth-century America. It must involve the postulation and facilitation of new and multiple approaches to the enrichment of individual lives and to enhanced social justice.

For Americans living in the last quarter of the twentieth century, what are the bedrock realities of human existence? Barring natural or man-made catastrophes, are they not three?

First, most Americans born in the latter half of the twentieth century, if they take even reasonable care of themselves, will live substantially beyond the biblically allotted years of three-score and ten. Medical breakthroughs—especially in the treatment of heart disease, cancer, and stroke—are beginning to extend expectations of life well beyond the actuarial plateau that has maintained for most of this century in the Western world. However brief this candle may seem when viewed by the eye of eternity, a life span of seventy-five to eighty years involves a massive 650,000 to 700,000 hours of being, which is a lot of hours although not necessarily a lot of being. Even if sleep is deducted, something close to a half-million waking hours will be experienced by most Americans over their life span. Although the details of existence for the individual are unpredictable and highly variegated, one existential proposition can be made with a probability approaching certitude: everyone will experience changes—most of them highly predictable—in physical capabilities and psychological attitudes in the process of maturing and aging. This is the bedrock reality of the *stages of development.*

For adult Americans, a second existential proposition will have substantial universality: waking hours will be spent in shifting combinations of personal and family coping, work, and free-self activities. Over sixty years of adult life, as the days and seasons roll, these repetitive preoccupations along with sleep will constitute for most people the bedrock reality of the *existential wheel.*

Third, each person will live out stages of development and spin an existential wheel within the context of a series of political, economic, and social systems. These systems will determine to great extent who will

Figure 1
Enveloping

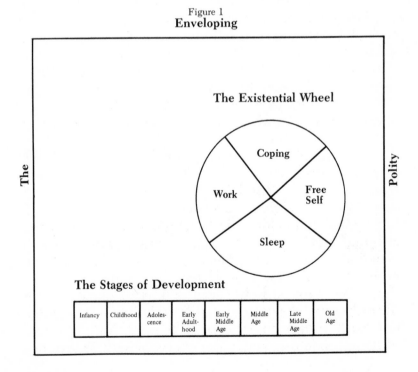

be employed; how goods and services will be distrib-
uted; the rate of inflation; the availability of health,
educational, and recreational services; the noxiousness
or felicity of urban life; the degree and stability of
international order; and a host of other conditions
that will directly affect the quality of individual lives.
This is the bedrock reality of the *enveloping polity.*

What if the diverse institutions and instruments that
constitute our educational system should consciously
address these bedrock realities with the following basic
purposes in mind:

> —to help persons anticipate, and increase their
> capacity for creative engagements with, major
> predictable changes—physical and psychologi-
> cal—in their stages of development;
> —to help persons in their concentric communities
> to cope, to work, and to use their free time in
> ways that minimize neurotic anxiety and boredom
> and that maximize inner fulfillment and joyful
> reciprocities;
> —to help persons to learn the arts of affecting the
> enveloping polity in order to promote justice and
> to secure the blessings of liberty for others as
> well as for themselves.

For anyone who begins such speculations, as I do,
from a familial and cultural background in democratic
political theory and liberal Protestantism, such summary formulations of basic educational purposes bring
more initial comfort than closer examination affords.
Each of the three propositions skims over some of
history's toughest philosophical issues:

> —What is the good life?
> —Has reason the power to lead toward the approxi-
> mation of the good life?
> —When "goods" conflict, what justifies the choice
> of one against others?
> —Except in preoccupations with perceived crisis,

are persons doomed to discontent? (Or, on the other hand, are discontents about to dissolve in the sedations and euphorias of experimental pharmacology?)

—Does the sense and reality of community emerge as an escape from individual fears of loneliness and estrangement, or from a natural gregariousness?

—In Yeats's terms, is there an irreconcilable competition between "perfection of work" and "perfection of life"?

—In the tensions between equality and quality, what beyond the status of the observer can determine an optimized admixture of the two?

—How much of human happiness is genetically conditioned?

—If justice is equity, who determines it? On the other hand, if justice is "the interest of the stronger" and if liberty is the right of the strong to do what they will, who except the strong needs either justice or liberty?

That this essay refrains from an explication of its three existential propositions in relation to these and similar philosophical dilemmas is not to denigrate such inquiry. It is to return to the image of focal distance. (Professor E. E. Schattschneider once said that if a hill is examined with a microscope, it disappears.) It is also to repair to a personal belief that however mysterious the universe, and however hopeful or tragic the ultimate human condition may be *sub specie aeternitatis*, the quality of existential being and the norms and behaviors of social institutions are in some measure malleable.

Man's hope, as against unyielding fate, is grounded in more than whim, although it falters in the face of ultimate why's. For example, the human condition was improved, in my estimation, with the invention of modern anesthetics. But why the absence of pain is generally better than the presence of pain is an evidentiary problem, and involves a value preference, capable of rational elaboration but not of rational proof. In the resolution of social conflicts, I believe with Winston Churchill that "jaw-jaw is better than war-war," although once again the ultimate justification for this position is a matter of value preference that rests on multiple observations of consequences. If someone asks why violence, carnage, fear, hysteria, and trauma are worse than their absence or opposite, my answer must be, I have witnessed both, and under most circumstances the latter appear to be more compatible with human dignity and fulfillment—at least for the many—than are the former. Why human dignity and fulfillment are worth the trouble evokes commitments of faith and affection beyond rationality.

These assumptions and value preferences lead, for purposes of this essay, to interconnected propositions: There is more misery in the world than need be, and education broadly conceived can do something about this condition. The internalization of the idea that the quality of life can be improved contains a powerful dynamic. The belief that the educational system broadly conceived constitutes a major agent of amelioration gives that dynamic an instrumental focus.

It may be argued that any definition of the educational system so broad as to include social institutions and facilities beyond those associated with formal schooling is too complex for clinical analysis or therapeutic utility. But many compelling denials of this argument have been made. Since Plato (and perhaps before), most political and educational theorists (frequently they have been the same) have postulated educational programs and systems far beyond schools, classrooms, and laboratories. The education of Plato's Guardians, for example, included years of "middle-management" experience. In the early days of the Roman Republic, the chief educational agency was not the school but the home. Pliny the Younger spoke

for a world and for times beyond his ken when he
wrote that it was an ancient custom "that we should
learn from our elders, not only through the ear but
also through the eye, those things that we should soon
have to do, and in our turn hand them down to our
successors." Lawrence A. Cremin has lined out in
exquisite detail the variety of educative instruments—
including churches, apprenticeships, literary societies—that have informed our growth as a people and
as a nation.

Actually, the very size and scope of our educational
resources are harbingers of hope. The points of lever-
age are multiple. In many cases the most powerful
instruments for dealing with certain kinds of human
experience may well be other than formal institutions
of schools, colleges, and universities. Sometimes answers may be found in more effective articulation of
one segment of schooling to another, or of formal
schooling to other less formal educative instruments
and agents in the society.

The chapters ahead explore ways in which the major
educative instruments in the American society may
relate more effectively than in the past to the bedrock
existential realities of the stages of development, the
existential wheel, and the enveloping polity.

2

Education and the Stages of Development

Nothing in human experience is more certain than that people grow, age, and die. From the Greek riddle of the four-, two-, and three-legged animal, through Shakespeare's seven ages of man and Kierkegaard's "stages on life's way," to the most recent investigations into the psychology and physiology of growth and aging, observers have noticed regularities in the unfolding transitions of human lives.

In the twentieth century, major credit for opening up important aspects of the life-cycle to both systematic observation and intuitive speculation must go to Carl G. Jung, Charlotte Bühler, and Erik Erikson. Jung's early essay on "The Stages of Life" is a classic in the field. Bühler's empirical work in Austria, beginning in the 1930's, was central to the evolution of the concept. Erikson's writings, and his famous course on the human life cycle at Harvard, brought one of the century's most sensitive and creative psychoanalytic minds to bear upon the repetitive realities of human existence. In recent years, a number of talented American psychologists, sociologists, medical scientists, and educators have joined Erikson in addressing empirical, analytical, and intuitive aspects of human growth and aging. The specialized field of the cognitive development of the young, of course, has had as its master the great Swiss psychologist, Jean Piaget. While many American psychologists have been concerned with cognitive changes over the years of maturity, a growing number of behavioral scientists have addressed the stages of development as a psychophysical unity involving far more than shifts in cognitive capabilities.

There is little mystery to the belatedness of the attention that scientists and humanists have given to studies of the human life cycle. Until the twentieth century, biblically allotted spans of life were only for a hardy few. Part of the traditional veneration of the old was a function of their scarcity. However, in the technologically advanced parts of the Western world, since the turn of the twentieth century, life expectancy has virtually doubled. Even if the toll of childhood diseases is discounted, life expectancy has increased substantially. This dramatic shift is a partial fulfillment of Bernard Shaw's prediction that an assumed long span of years was the precondition of human beings taking life seriously. That long span of years, assuming an absence of holocausts, is now with us.

Although a number of alternative schemata exist for delineating the human stages of development, the Eriksonian model is a useful archetype.

In *Childhood and Society,* Erikson posits eight "stages of man," four in the period before puberty, four including and following puberty. He believes that each stage is marked by competing psychological responses to the interplay of the physical organism, the individual ego (as the organizer of experience), and the surrounding environment. He calls his eight stages:

—Basic trust vs. mistrust (oral states)
—Autonomy vs. shame and doubt (anal stages)
—Initiative vs. guilt (pregenital state)
—Industry vs. inferiority (prepuberty)
—Identity vs. role confusion (adolescence)
—Intimacy vs. isolation (young adulthood)

—Generativity vs. stagnation (mature adulthood)
—Ego integrity vs. despair (old age)

Erikson's rich mind recognizes the ambiguities of language and the arbitrariness of categories. But as Robert Coles has pointed out in his intellectual biography of Erikson, the great psychoanalyst believes that the tentative coherence of his point of view has utility in stimulating further thought.

As Erikson would be the first to assert, the science of life-cycle development has been questioned, and some of his disciples have suggested alternative systems. And some critics have expressed doubts that any tight typology tied to the passage of particular years, or even to the general idea of life-cycle linearity, can be proved, so variable are individual makeups; so accidental, culture bound, and intermittent are congeries of experiences producing human stress; so persistent the psychological manifestations of idiosyncratic childhood or even genetic factors.

The position of these critics seems to me extreme. Granted variations in the precise timing of biological clocks and externally determined life adjustments, and of individual reactions to both, most people in twentieth-century America grow, mature, and age according to roughly standard calendars, and an overwhelming majority of American adults appear to face roughly similar psychological stresses as they confront recurring crises of identity and expectation. In any case, precision in distinguishing specific stages of development is not germane to the main thrust of this essay on educational purposes. Two derivative propositions, however, are:

1) The quality of early nurture mightily affects the future organism and personality;
2) A number of highly predictable life-cycle adjustments of the sort identified by Erikson are traumatic for large numbers of people.

If appropriate educational experiences could be designed to increase the capacity of parents, older siblings, day-care personnel, social workers, visiting nurses, and teachers to understand and to foster conditions favorable to the healthy development of infants and children, a vast amount of human misery might ultimately be alleviated. And if various parts of the educational system at appropriate times and places, and with a variety of pedagogic techniques, increased the capacity of people to have creative engagements with the most predictable traumas of the postpuberty stages of development, the sum total of human happiness might be substantially enhanced.

Education and Early Nurture

Consider briefly some of the educational implications of proposition one: that the quality of early nurture mightily affects the future organism and personality. The following statements appear to be widely agreed upon among psychologists and pediatricians:

—The genetic code from both parents and the prenatal diet, drug habits, and health conditions of mothers can have important effects on the intellectual, emotional, and physical development of children.
—Frequent demonstrations of affection by adults and various forms of play (including activity involving ministresses) are important to an infant's cognitive and affective growth.
—Child neglect on the one hand, or excessively punitive reactions by adults to infant behavior on the other, can have traumatic effects for the victims.
—Encouraging children to fantasize can have a positive effect on their later capacity to be creative, to socialize, and to deal with stress.
—As the child's ego emerges, the capacity of parents

to create a nurture midground between anarchy and repression is a positive force toward assuring a socially responsible and self-reliant adult.

—A new child in the house can cause jealousy among those whose affections and attention patterns are thereby changed.

—Both the separation and divorce of parents, on the one hand, and prolonged open warfare between husband and wife on the other, tend to have a disruptive effect on a child's emotional integrity and to produce emotional scar tissue for the future.

—The cognitive capacity of children emerges in set stages, and unless pedagogy is aware of these stages, teaching can be either wasted or damaging.

Each of these propositions is subject to definitional and descriptive disagreements among experts, but they are supported by a high degree of professional consensus. Each, containing seeds for a rich garden of learning, could find its way into various school, college, and professional curricula, as well as into adult education of all kinds. Yet the learning must focus on those who set the environment within which the child develops—particularly parents but including older siblings and an extensive range of those presently performing custodial and pedagogic functions for the young.

An important instrumental purpose of education may therefore be stated in the following terms: to assist those responsible for the birth or nurturing of children in understanding the agents and conditions of optimal child development.

A moment's reflection, however, suggests the presence of a troublesome initial assumption underlying this statement of instrumental purpose: that those who transmit life or assume the burdens of nurture understand the solemnity of the responsibility and are committed to making sacrifices and to undergoing

behavior modifications in the interests of a child's
healthy maturation. This image of a near-universal
baptismal consecration bears little resemblance to
known biological and social reality: that most children
are born simply because sex is compulsively pleasurable; that the crying, the mess, and the safety surveillances of early childhood are in many cases for many
parents (especially mothers) a relentless burden; that
the condition of a child's sound growth may mean
adult sacrifices of confinements, foregone pleasures,
and marital tensions that, for many, can be all but
unbearable; that many day-care workers and nursery-
school teachers find television a tireless "baby-sitter"
that relieves them of the strains and the tedium of
pedagogical intervention.

For parents, of course, there are extraordinary
compensations: the erotic rewards of being suckled,
the parental joys of celebrating together the stages
of infant maturation, the ego rewards and nuzzling
intimacies of infant dependency and trust, the infec-
tiousness of irrepressible glee, the absolutely core and
lasting psychic rewards to adults of loving and being
loved by another human being, the temple satisfaction
of carrying out ancestral consecrations. But without
a strong sense of obligation and of devotional priority,
appropriate attention by relevant adults to the earliest
years of the stages of development of their charges
is fitful at best. And if the mores of a society lean,
as those in America presently do, toward self-indulgence and immediate gratification, the degree of fit-
fulness increases exponentially.

It is essential, therefore, to consider an educational
system for early childhood that assumes and tolerates
intermittencies and differing intensities in adult commitment. Fortunately, four contemporary social trends
are helping to point the way: family planning, the
women's liberation movement, the day-care and nursery-school movements, and the rediscovery of the
social utility of older citizens.

With the advent of a variety of effective techniques of birth control, couples can, for the first time in human history, make rational choices about whether or not to have children, and, if so, how many and when. These choices give parents an opportunity to relate child bearing to the improvement of child development.

"Women's liberation" in the minds of traditionalists is more a part of the problem than a part of the solution. Children, it is argued, are increasingly neglected because mothers want to be "freed" from housework including child rearing. But this line of argument is far from the necessary logic of the women's liberation movement. A more felicitous projection is a world in which men and women are brought up in the assumption that child rearing and general housework are mutual enterprises; that the man spells the woman, and vice versa, in handling the drudgery and protective surveillances of childhood—as well as the cooking, cleaning, shopping, and bed-making. The restructuring of traditional divisions of labor and role assignments is compatible with evolving images of human dignity, opening up the possibility that both parents will have been educated and experienced in sound principles of child rearing.

All of this, of course, involves child nurture in the evenings and on the weekends. But if both parents work, who looks after the child during the day? Many European countries are far ahead of the United States in providing day-care and nursery-school opportunities for the children of working parents. Even so, a large number of day-care centers and nursery schools exist in America: an estimated 20,000 of the former and 50,000 of the latter. Furthermore, there are more than 60,000 licensed day-care homes and countless informal arrangements for neighborhood "kiddie pools" of various sorts and sizes. Conservatively, something like two million young children spend parts of each day with parental surrogates. Looking ahead, the studied development of educational opportunities and materials in the field of child rearing for these parental surrogates could have an important and salutary impact on the education of the children themselves. As kibbutz experience has demonstrated, for example, expertly led group experiences can have a healthy socializing effect on children and can contribute substantially to their capacity for cooperation as adults.

A considerable extension of day-care and nursery-school opportunities for the children of working parents is, of course, a matter of social priorities. But many way-stations can exist between a comprehensive national policy and the present kaleidoscope of federal programs and local public and private services heavily biased toward the interests of the affluent. One of these way-stations might well be the mobilization of older citizens in the cause of childhood education and of child rearing generally. Schools of education and schools of human development could well provide extension services for training and retraining retired people to prepare them for a variety of educative tasks associated with child rearing. On a volunteer or part-time basis, older citizens so trained could move back into a mainstream of usefulness. A triple social good would result: for the relieved parent, for the served child, and for the sense of worth of the older citizen.

These, then, are examples of ways in which the concept of life stages can serve as a focus for speculations about educational purposes. Infancy and early childhood are critically important stages in the life cycle. The cliché is precise: "As the twig is bent. . . ." Curricular changes in schools and colleges, as well as new outreach programs to educate those who educate the young, might do much to improve the life chances of children. Family planning, the women's liberation movement, the day-care and nursery-school movements, and the rediscovery of the social utility of older people are modern trends that show promise of stimulating educational attention to sound child development. To these must, of course, be added the hope that, for many, traditional family commitments and satisfactions will maintain or resume their historic importance.

Some Educational Implications of Life-Cycle Anxieties

Turning to the educational implications of Erikson's work on adolescent and adult stages of development, three examples may suffice to suggest the richness of the possibilities.

All the major students of the life cycle identify adolescence—especially late adolescence—as a particularly troublesome period for everyone concerned. This perception conforms, of course, to the common experience of most Americans in this century. Such cultural and temporal qualifications are important, for the traumas of adolescence appear to be muted in situations where the need of families, and of the economy generally, for adolescent services is patent and pressing (for example, agriculture, fishing). In the late twentieth century in the United States, most young people in their teens are urban dwellers, are consumers rather than producers of goods and services, are barely tolerated in the labor market, and are highly dependent on those they are psychologically increasingly ready (even eager) to quit.

During the 1960s, a vast literature emerged attempting to illuminate the giddy behaviors and gothic anxieties of American adolescents—including some significant essays by Erikson himself. In retrospect, the Russian roulette of the Vietnam draft was heavily responsible for what Erikson has called the "intensified adolescence" of the 1960s. Even without the peculiar anxieties prompted by the war, American young people would have undergone the trauma of attenuated adolescence. And the unhealthy reality continues. Although street crime and major felonies

perpetrated by the young continue to climb disturbingly, much of the physical violence associated with
the campus activities of the 1960s has subsided.
Unfortunately, manifestations of *psychic* violence—
including psychic flagellation—continue ominously.
Seemingly unable to cope with the ego bruises of
intimacy, all too many young people wander aimlessly
in a limbo of contentiousness, self-pity, drug fixes,
and shrugging detachment. They develop Faustian
compulsions for experiencing everything, but in a
non-Faustian time frame of immediacy. There is irony
in youth attempting to stuff all experience, no matter
how exotic and bizarre, into the tiny time capsule
of late adolescence when, for the first time in human
history, they have six or seven decades in front of
them. Why has this happened?

Plausible explanations abound:

—the peaking of an unprecedented adolescent age
cohort produced by the post-World War II baby
boom;

—physical maturity occurring earlier but adult roles
further postponed, leaving adolescents in an attenuated psychic and functional limbo;

—the breakdown in commonly held systems of moral
and aesthetic values, a breakdown that deprives
young people, among other things, of accepted
bench marks for judging the "outrageousness" of
deviations;

—anxieties attendant upon the dissolution of traditional functions of, and obligations within, the
family;

—the "over-completedness" of society, the sense that
the system is too ponderous and cynical to accommodate idealistic and creative modifications by
the young;

—disillusionment following the assassination of the
two Kennedys and of Martin Luther King, Jr.,
in the 1960s; cynicism following Watergate in
the 1970s;

—the sense, noted above, of not being needed by
   the economy except in menial and dead-end jobs;
—the macabre caricature of reality emanating from
   TV, and the deadening passivity induced by
   watching TV;
—the fragmentation of the psyche resulting from
   the barrage of stimuli unleashed by wanton technologies of sound and motion;
—the absence of positive role-models that contain
   both adventure and security;
—the anxiety of constantly facing a myriad of
   lackluster options;
—the knowledge-rich, action-poor biases of the present educational system, especially in the last two
   years of high school;
—and, for the poor and discriminated against, the
   oppressive recognition of class and caste and
   of being the victims of loaded dice.

All of these dissonances are today superimposed
upon the normal strains of adolescent adjustment: the
onset of puberty, the painful winnowing of childhood
compulsions, the growing resentment toward parental
authority, the search for self, the anxiety of loneliness
in the matrix of group conformity.

In this unsettled context, would not an appropriate
instrumental educational purpose be to help adolescents, and those who interact with them, to understand
the reasons for attenuated adolescent traumas, and to
explore ways of dealing creatively with those realities
that exacerbate inevitable adolescent anxieties?

There are moments when such a postulation must
seem a chimera, for the forces adversely affecting
American adolescents come close to describing a montage of the modern world. The tragedy of adolescence
may well be, in fact, the tragedy of an epoch. Furthermore, many steps that might be taken to ameliorate
the plight of the adolescent (for example, early job
opportunities) might well run afoul of adult-vested
interests too entrenched for negotiation.

But once again, there are positive as well as negative portents and possibilities. Changes are beginning to take place in the organization of work, changes that provide images of the future far friendlier to the adolescents' projections than are today's job patterns. Secondary schools are increasingly taking steps to reform the content of the twelfth grade and to provide career-related and other activity exposures and role-model contacts likely to brighten adolescent perceptions and options. Watergate ended in a triumph for the American constitutional system. Campaign funding has become more democratized, and a variety of consumer interests have been protected against well-entrenched industrial privilege and bureaucratic inertia. Millions of young people have rediscovered the beauty and the sanctity of nature, and through "problem-solving" high school and college classes, a few have actually participated creatively in finding solutions to local ecological insults. Perhaps most reassuring of all, millions of adolescents seem to weather the storms of this troubled stage without any more obvious effects than a slight queasiness from passing turbulence. In fact, the heightening of the adolescent trauma by current cultural forces seems, in many cases, to strengthen the will of some young people to create, not simply new semi-isolated communities but new life-styles, new loyalties, new relationships, and new bastions of psychic independence within existing communities.

These signs of promise do not, however, mean that all is well. The conditions of modern adolescence noted earlier are widespread. Parents; teachers; curricular supervisors; counselors; governmental, economic, and religious leaders; recreational directors; police; doctors; social workers; media programmers; and other interactors with youth have every reason, separately and jointly, to create and undertake educational programs and experiences that address the traumas in the adolescent stage of the American life cycle. And involving young people themselves as full partners in this task may be more therapeutic for them, and ultimately for society, than any single remedy discovered or invented along the way.

Students of the life cycle are generally agreed on another critical phase of human development in the contemporary American cultural setting. Erikson calls it the stage of "mature adulthood"; Bühler refers to it as the "climacterum." It hits most people in their forties and fifties, and is marked by physiological changes: in women, by menopause; in men, by hair loss; in both sexes, by weakening of the eyes. Psychologically, the stage has a variety of manifestations. Erikson refers to the polar conditions as "generativity" vs. "stagnation." For those who are capable of creative engagements with the stresses of middle age, it can be a period of maximum accomplishment and productivity. For too many people, it is a period of depression and drift. A favorite topic of women's magazines and of soap operas, the stereotypes of middle age have become part of the cultural landscape:

—the bored housewife, children grown, neurotic about the hot flashes of menopause;
—the slowed-down businessman who suddenly realizes that he will never make vice president of the company and that the rest of his working life will be a succession of inane repetitions;
—vanity-panics in both sexes as paunches began to protrude and the will to contain them recedes;
—a sudden sense of mortality and existential futility, often accompanied by graceless chasing after sexual reassurances;
—drinking more and enjoying it less;
—lingering with the horror of the morning mirror;
—an ineffable *Weltschmertz*, loneliness, and sense that "I'm no damn good."

To pretend that there are educational solutions to all these debilitating manifestations of middle age is

to trivialize egregious aspects of human existence. As
in the case of adolescence, some of the traumas of
middle age are hurts too deep for known therapy.
Furthermore, for some manifestations of the climacterum, medicines may be far more appropriate and
effective instruments of psychological health than
experiments in education.

Yet we in America have really never attempted to
design an educational system among whose major
purposes it is to help people anticipate, and have
creative engagements with, the known, predictable
stresses of middle age. Some adult-education movements have sensed the void of leisure time, and have
proferred a smörgasbord of afternoon and evening
classes and workshops available to the middle-aged
as to persons of all ages. Undergraduate liberal-arts
curricula have been justified, in part, as providing
people with a sufficient "furniture of the mind" (a
favorite nineteenth-century phrase) to give them the
grace and internal resources for dealing with life's
adversities and perversities—presumably including
the stresses of the climacterum. But apart from the
plethora of pseudoscientists and homilists who crowd
the pages of journalistic ephemera, few attempts are
made in the American society to reflect on the crises
of middle age as a specific educational challenge.

This lack is easily accounted for. Most people still
hold to the stereotype of education as formal schooling
and as taking place in the first quarter of a person's
life. Furthermore, systematic knowledge about the
physiological and psychological stresses of middle age
is only now beginning to emerge in a form that is
generalizable, prognostic, and potentially the basis for
therapy. Finally, most of the discomforts have been
deemed by most people to be incurable, a judgment
that if wrong by as much as 25 percent ought to prompt
creative thought and studied experimentation among
concerned educators.

How and where could education designed to combat

the stresses of middle age be developed and offered? High school and college curricula could certainly be adjusted to accommodate courses and modules specifically addressed to such matters. One dividend of developments at this level might well be heightened understanding by adolescents and young adults of parental behavior and of ways in which young people could help ease rather than exacerbate parental anxieties. The major educational intervention, however, must come just prior to and during the climacterum itself. Formal, highly directed educational offerings by extension divisions of colleges and universities; informal seminars organized by churches and synagogues, women's clubs and service clubs, industries and unions—all of these could well be fostered with this educational purpose in mind. A few experiments are already under way. It is, however, highly probable that, for many middle-aged adults, the traumas of the climacterum produce the very kinds of anxiety that are least negotiable in formal, group-learning environments. The threats of psychic exposure are simply too painful; even the motivation and energy needed to "get to class" may not be available.

Special attention, therefore, must be given to the superior education of the people who are most likely to be in positions to help those who need help through the wildernesses of this penultimate life stage: especially doctors, visiting nurses, psychiatrists, educational counselors, social workers, lawyers, and clergy. Both preservice and, especially, inservice training should be available that would help the capacity of these professionals to understand the diagnostics, prognostics, and therapeutics of the predictable stresses of the climacterum. In addition, both TV and audiotapes and videotapes offer extraordinary opportunities for reaching those suffering the peculiar traumas of middle age—and with the benign lack of threat that home-oriented telecommunications provide. Finally, books and articles that go beyond the banalities of pseudobehavioral science and the easy euphorias of prescriptive psychic and religious conversions will continue to play an important educational role—for helpers as well as for those needing help (they are frequently the same).

Finally, there is the largely unexplored frontier of education for old age. Seneca's aphorism is a statement of the obvious: "Old age and happiness are frequently strangers." There is no set time for the onset of old age, although it is often associated with retirement from the labor market. The signs are easily identifiable: the death or degenerative illness of a relative or close friend of approximately the same age; an increase in aches and pains; the tendency of others to mumble their words and of publishers of phone books to reduce the type size.

And then for all too many comes the running of a gauntlet. In increasing numbers, contemporaries vanish. The structure of meaning associated with one's work suddenly disappears. Depreciated income precludes much of the fun of retirement. One's spouse develops a terminal illness and then disappears forever, leaving a desperate void until the calluses of existential indifference form their benign numbness. Children, caught up in their own affairs, call and write less frequently. One's own health degenerates in slipped cogs and discs. The association with other elderly people often in impersonal institutional settings is a depressant. As long as sight and hearing last, television is both a godsend and a bore. Pain, at least, is a distraction from loneliness. Death turns out not to be a bad fellow after all. One day the loneliness ends in the endlessly creative plasma of the universe.

It is idle to pretend that educational interventions can overcome all of the vicissitudes of old age. But old age does not have to be as doleful as the above threnody implies. Even if—as is unlikely—gerontological medicine fails to progress, and even if social policies with respect to the relationship of the aged to the job market remain archaic, a wide variety of educational endeavors could still materially dispel some of the gloom associated with advanced years. Among other things, earlier studies purporting to prove the inevitable decline of learning capacities as a result of aging have been largely discredited. *Lifelong* education can now be reasonably expected to be consonant with *long-life* education.

Once again the insertion of modules about aging into secondary and postsecondary curricula might at least increase the understanding of young people and young adults, and help them to help older relatives and neighbors over the bumps of advancing years. The long-range effects of harmful drugs, unbalanced diets, and physical laziness during the first three-quarters of the cycle on the quality of existence during the last quarter is a continuing theme that should be featured, first, during the years of formal schooling, but repeated through a variety of educative agencies. As William James once pointed out, the drunk may argue that "this one won't count," but, alas, "the molecules count it" and revenge takes its worst toll, not in the form of shortened life, but as prolonged misery. Studies conducted at the University of California at Los Angeles by Lester Breslow indicate a clear relationship between good health habits and increased longevity. "The daily habits of people," Dr. Breslow claims, "have a great deal more to do with what makes them sick and when they die than all the influences of medicine."

The most important educational contributions to old age, as it is lived, must be made as in the case of the climacterum, just prior to and during the phase itself. In one sense the capacity to enjoy creative engagements with the stresses of old age is a function of a person's entire previous life viewed as "education." Nevertheless, a variety of educational opportunities and materials could be aimed at the predictable needs of the aging just before and after retirement begins. Some industries, unions, and professional organizations already provide various forms of pre- and postretirement assistance. Far more could be done. Colleges and universities have a special obligation and opportunity to use surplus dormitory spaces and slack pedagogical plants to meet the varied learning needs and possibilities of the aged. Medical personnel, clergy, and social workers need to find ways of using their opportunities for interventions to instruct their older clients in the hazards and coping-skills that are related to getting along in years.

The instrumental purpose in such education should not be to obliterate all trauma associated with growing older. It should be to maximize for an appreciable and increasing percentage of elderly the chance that they will reflect the hoary Chinese in Yeats's *Lapis Lazuli:*

> . . . their eyes,
> Their ancient, glittering eyes are gay.

3

Coping

Barring catastrophes, for the sixty or so years of their adult existence, most Americans will live out each week engaged in a series of highly repetitive activities. The mix of these activities will shift with time and obligation, but for most people at least half of the 168 hours in each week will be spent in either sleep or in the often mean and petty business of existential coping. Education may not have much influence on the quality of sleep, but it could have an impressive effect on the quality of existential coping—including sleeplessness.

By existential coping, I refer to performing those biological functions, completing those logistical tasks, and wrestling with those psychic dissonances that accompany the very fact of being alive in a functioning sense. Patently, existential coping is no issue for the comatose.

Most adult Americans spend a substantial part of each week in the following kinds of activities: preparing food, eating it, and cleaning up afterwards; brushing teeth; going to the toilet; washing bodies and clothes; shopping, repairing machines (or having them repaired); paying bills; balancing accounts; banking; going to, or worrying about the need to go to, doctors, dentists, and lawyers; filling out insurance and tax forms; fulfilling mandatory, expected, or hoped-for roles vis-a-vis spouses, children, other relatives and intimates, the community, and the law; parrying the anguishes of self-image, illness, nuclear threats, and relationships with others and with the universe. These things go on whether one is employed or not, retired or not, married or single. They constitute for most people the very stuff of mundane existence.

Parts of the daily routine are psychically neutral, even pleasurable. For some people, chores like shopping and cooking are not chores at all, but a real delight. For all too many, too much of the time, however, the coping segment of the existential wheel is sullen, frustrating, and anxiety ridden. On some days it is excruciating: glasses are misplaced, the car won't start, the dog dirties the rug, the earache gets worse, accounts won't balance, the express line at both the bank and the supermarket turns out to be the slow line, the motor vehicle department returns the auto registration form for additional information, the spouse is cantankerous, the kids quarrelsome, the weather lugubrious.

In the early 1950s, two commission reports on the subject appeared under the title *Life Adjustment for Youth.* The phrase was unfortunate, the contents often naive or complacent. But the reports rested on an important premise: that education should make some useful contribution to the recurring realities of adult existence. When slaves bore the brunt of logistical coping, as they did in ancient Greece, Plato and Aristotle could afford to address their educational theories to the more elevated aspects of human consciousness: to leisure and statecraft. In twentieth-century America, education has failed to prepare most young people and adults to master the day-to-day coping problems of life.

It seems obvious that no combination of educational programs made available through family tutelage, new curricula in schools or colleges, adult extension and counseling services, the mass media, or otherwise, will make existential coping euphoric. The cussedness of inanimate objects and the variations, convolutions, and contentious chemistries of psyches set an outer limit to ameliorative tinkering. There are, nevertheless, four areas of existential coping that probably lend themselves to substantial improvement through appropriate education—improvement in increasing the capacity of the individual to substitute a degree of mastery for the slogging frustrations and nagging anxieties that becloud so much of existence. The four areas are: illness, personal and family logistics, psychological misunderstandings, and the search for meaning. The educational system is dotted with longstanding efforts as well as promising experiments touching on most of these areas. Yet effective educational preparation for existential coping is still inadequate as judged by the evidences of frustration, estrangement, psychic violence, and anguish that combine to depress so much of American life.

Illness

For something that is impossible to define, good health for most Americans is still an inescapable issue. In a superficial sense, good health is the absence of physical aches, pains, and discomforts, and the consciousness of adequate energy and of unimpaired senses. But some people who "feel fine" may be dying of an insidious malady; others who test normal may have vague phlegms that make them miserable. Anyone who has chased hypoglycemia or various psychosomatic illnesses around their elusive courses recognizes the reality of the latter point. Looking ahead, computer-assisted diagnostics and therapy based on chemical fine-tuning may come to reduce such discomforts to a minimum. Meantime, these miseries, along with more obvious and testable illnesses, will take an enormous toll. Americans are now spending more than $100 billion a year on health services and supplies. For the elderly, illness is a major concern and a ubiquitous topic of conversation.

Increased knowledge about the nature of illness and the conditions of good health may not, of course, actually result in changed human behavior. One great frustration in the medical profession is the propensity of patients to ignore doctors' orders. Warnings of the Surgeon General are ignored by tens of millions of smokers. Taking nonethical drugs, getting drunk, and staying fat—however taxing on key human organs—are often the self-administered therapies for life's unbearables, and are not easily monitored and abjured by pallid superegos. Living in large cities is probably prejudicial to physical well-being, but no massive exodus is evident (or, for many people, possible). Fats and carbohydrates are important ingredients of a balanced diet, but they can be physiologically vicious when predominant—and predominant they are in the American menu. Regular exercise in moderation is a known plus in the creation and maintenance of bodily health, but millions of Americans follow the late Alexander Woollcott in his practice, when feeling like exercise, of lying down until the feeling goes away. And, alas, in the deep recesses of some psyches are compulsions toward flagellation, or insatiable hungers for pity and attention commanded by sickness, that defy Aristotelian logic. For such people are both sick and well at the same time, and the sicker they get, the "weller" they feel. There are, of course, genetic and environmental factors that may produce dread illnesses even in those who have treated their bodies like temples.

Simply giving people health information—through schools, books, articles, or public-service advertising—will obviously never automatically change their health habits and conditions. But to doubt an immediate millenium is not to deny the possibility of progress. The educational system broadly conceived should have as one of its essential instrumental purposes the improvement of health. Education can contribute through the advanced training of bioscientists, medical personnel, public health specialists, and environmental engineers. Possibly more important, education, by addressing the broader lay population, can work on the internalization of the pathological consequences of repetitive insults to the human system—even though many people will take no heed. On a cost/benefit basis, billions spent in preventive medicine and health education would probably do far more for the sense and reality of physical well-being of Americans of all ages than the same amount spent on direct medical care. Surely, the ultimate goal of public policy should be to reduce the need for medical care by promoting and underwriting preventive medicine.

Health is a basic human concern and, at all stages of the life cycle, every possible facet of the educational system must be involved in its improvement. For better or worse, by precept or example, the family is the fundamental health educator. Schools are doing a good deal through courses (often state-required) and modules in personal health care, and through physical education classes and sports. A variety of privately and community-sponsored recreational programs and playgrounds, and for many young people summer camps, are useful educative instruments. Occupational safety and health has been a vital concern of many industries and unions, and is the subject of important federal legislation. District nurses, social workers, and clergy can be and frequently are important health educators. Even more should be done by all of these instruments and agents. And far more attention to making health education and physical education attractive to the students of our colleges and universities is needed. It is poor life preparation to spend all day with a book, stereo, radio, or television set.

The new frontiers of health education, however, involve the health professions themselves and the use of the mass media—including especially cable TV and videotapes or videoplatters. One of the shortcomings of modern medicine in the United States is the absence of effective two-way vertical communication linking research to clinical practice, and horizontal communication by which successful practice in one clinic or region can be adapted to similar medical needs in other clinics or regions. Also serious is the uneven use of technology in diagnosing and treating illness. These are not insuperable hiatuses. They are susceptible to multiple educational approaches by medical schools, communications researchers, information-retrieval experts, and media specialists. At some time in the future, two-way telecommunications in the home may offer remarkable opportunities for improving health care in underserved rural areas and overcrowded urban centers.

Because health is an important problem among older people, all parts of the educative system should give special attention to the health habits of those in their fifties and early sixties. The root motivation to prolong life tends to increase its intensity during this period. Bodies abused directly or insidiously over decades begin to manifest isolated protests. At this point, the body is still regenerative enough so that changes in habits may have a felicitous effect on the corroding attenuations of old age. Medical personnel can, if they will, become key educators for this age cohort. But they will need the reinforcement of all the educative instruments and personnel that have the capacity to influence adult perceptions and behaviors, including the purveyors of the homilies of early schooling. In all this, it is wise to remember the insight of Cyril O. Houle that "nobody is interested in health but everybody is interested in illness."

Personal and Family Logistics

Except, perhaps, for those expertly trained in both accountancy and motorcycle maintenance, the ordinary logistics associated with living in a complex, technological, bureaucratic society are frequently baffling and maddening. Education does little to help. Some argue that this is as it should be. But if the Catch-22s of logistical coping are both time-consuming and anxiety-producing, why should the educational system not accept as a legitimate purpose a heightened logistical efficiency for all people? If pedagogically well organized, education for logistical coping should not consume substantial time. Some of it could take place as written and laboratory exercises tied to more general and theoretical learning; some of it could be facilitated by speakers brought into schools and colleges or, through TV, into the home. Some of it is as simple as a visit to a public library or a postcard to the U.S. Government Printing Office.

For anyone old enough to have experienced over several years the frustrations associated with logistical coping, examples come readily if unhappily to mind.

First of all, there are the myriad irritations associated with personal and family accounts: justifying bank statements, computing interest rates, filling out tax forms, monitoring insurance claims and payments, negotiating credit, making investments, constructing a reasonable personal or family financial plan. Mini-calculators have taken over some of the arithmetic drudgery. Yet without some education in the minimal tidiness of record keeping, some introduction to fine print, some supervised coping exercises, or some knowledge of where to obtain reasonably disinterested expert advice, millions of people are driven to distraction by the mundane mathematics of daily life. General courses in math are almost beside the point unless they include a considerable number of applied exercises. Many schools and colleges do offer good courses in business mathematics and useful modules in the finances of home management, but they tend to reach only a fraction of the students. Personal and family accounts are part of *all* American adult lives. The chores cannot be avoided. Through appropriate training, much of the attendant anxiety and frustration might be escaped.

What is true of accounts is also true of consumer economics. Comparative shopping takes time, and for

some temperaments and income levels it is a colossal
bore. For those living close to the margin, forced into
unemployment, or suffering the ravages of inflation,
however, a knowledge of weights and measures, sea-
sonal bargains, and label-reading may make a powerful
difference in the standard of living. Beyond shopping,
some educational exposure to, say, the ten most frequent malfunctions of automobile engines and television sets—symptoms, remedies, and if beyond practical repair at home, the probable fair cost of their being
fixed—might well save the American consumer from
frustrations and rip-offs. Knowledge of what to look
for in making large purchases (a car, real estate, major
insurance policies, a college education) should be
available in educational forms beyond the prejudices
of neighbors and the sales line of those with vested
interests. Again, in scattered examples, high school,
college, and adult education courses do focus on these
or related matters, but again, they touch only a tiny
proportion of the population.

Personal and family law constitutes another area
of popular ignorance that deserves educational illumi-
nation. The issue is not whether to turn everyone into
a "do-it-yourself" lawyer. To the contrary, the issue,
in part, is to help people judge when they need expert
legal opinion and help. Everyone should have at least
a rudimentary understanding of his legal rights as
a citizen, of torts and contracts, of marriage law and
probate law, of liability and its limits, and, especially,
some insights into changing concepts of property. In
a complex, largely urban society, a knowledge of the
legal matrix of personal and social existence should
be an important instrumental purpose of the educational system.

With few exceptions, educational attention to the
legal aspects of existential coping for the lay person
has been, until recently, a desert. Fortunately, in recent
years, some law schools, bar associations, private
foundations, and federal agencies have become cata-

lysts of scholastic, collegiate, and adult education
curricular and modular developments in this important
area. For the future citizen, substituting material in
usable law for social studies courses devoted to drawing seventeenth-century Indian trails would be, in
my estimation, a great forward step.

Psychological Misunderstandings

In spite of centuries of religious and philosophical
speculation and literary explication and analogy, and
in spite of the illuminations of Freud and his more
recent modifiers and antagonists, the inner life of
people is still an enigma. Even the term "inner life"
is embarrassingly fuzzy for, among other things, it
connotes a psychological dualism that may be non-
sense. Conceivably, the root properties of "human
nature" may never be known. A perverse "Heisenberg
uncertainty principle" may place the *workings* of the
human mind beyond the analytic—even analogic—
capacities of the human mind. We may never learn,
for example, how we learn. We may have to settle
for scientific shadows on the wall of Plato's cave—
mercurial shadows of language that "tell" us that the
mind is simply a bizarre congeries of partly programmed, partly random chemical interactions playing
on the memory cells of an organic computer. Such
formulations   may   have   heuristic,   pragmatic,
manipulable consequences for both education and
psychiatry, but as explanations of ultimate reality they
are on a par with primitive myths of creation and
are possibly well below Jungian and Oriental postu-
lates about the playful and diffusive creativity of the
"universal unconscious."

Again, however, for purposes of this essay "focal
distance" is important. Over several decades, the
psychologists and related behavioral scientists have
developed taxonomies, described recurring patterns
of behavior, and constructed clinical experiments that
substantially increase our knowledge about human

perceptions, motivations, anxieties, and aggressions.
The emerging theories, popularized and often corrupted in the process, have already had a perceptible
influence on the American culture. In many quarters,
for example, a raging "What a colossal bastard!" has
been transmuted into the shrug "So Joe is having an
ego-trip"; "My God, Jane is bitchy this morning!"
into "It must be that time of the month"; "Johnny
has suddenly become a monster," into "Johnny's new
brother just came home from the hospital."

The current propensity for lay psychologizing, however much of a rational surrogate for Christian charity,
may be unnerving the society's search for norms of
behavior. Yet norms, among other things, are needed
to shore up the identities and alleviate the miseries
of the very people whose manifest insecurities are
being explained and forgiven. To understand all is
to forgive all. But if forgiveness leads to too high
a tolerance for unsocial and antisocial behavior, demonic consequences are predictable. Satan's occupation may be willful cruelty, but his recreation is
anarchy.

Whatever the danger that heightened understanding
may lead to an unhealthy "permissiveness," such a
sequitur is by no means inevitable. It violates one
of psychology's most important concepts: the human
psyche's need for structure. The consequence of ignorance about human psychology is a world of endless
hurts, anxieties, and snarls. For young people to grow
up, and for adults to grow old, without understanding
that loneliness begins in the discreteness of birth and
the fear of death; that all psyches are insecure and
are as sensitive as an eyelash; that children who at
an early age are deprived of parents can become
stutterers; that prolonged fear is brutalizing; that
human sexuality has ramifications far beyond the
groin; that moods tend to be cyclical; that the traded
insults of intimacy—what R. D. Laing calls "psychic
binds"—are the "cheap shots" of injured egos; that

prolonged discrimination tends to rob people of the very confidence they need to prove the discriminators wrong; that in-groups strive to maintain turf, out-groups to penetrate it; that many behavioral feedback loops are observable and potentially liberating—to be ignorant of such psychological insights is to invite the dangers, miseries, and terrors of the unexamined life.

No aspect of psychological tensions needs more careful and sensitive exploration than the intimacies of family life. Marriage, child-parent, and sibling relationships are the oldest known constant in human history. The discords of intimacy constitute the basic drama of the Book of Genesis. Similar discords inform the themes of Greek tragedy, the portfolios of Shakespeare, the novels of Dostoyevsky, and the essays of Freud. The inability of humans to cope satisfactorily with those close to them may well be a root cause for aggressions committed against those living at greater distance.

Must of the dissonance of intimate family relationships was muted in the past by social and legal conventions that caused those victimized either to conform or to suffer punishment. Harsh as the punishments were, especially on women and children, they provided a framework of discipline and a system of manners that, in turn and in some measure, shielded the individual from the more brutal aspects of the ego onslaughts in family life. Because physical and legal escape for the injured was often difficult or impossible, great numbers of humans learned to grow calluses over their wounded egos and to cultivate bland stereotypic responses to insults hurled.

Twentieth-century mores have "liberated" individuals in a variety of ways. They can sulk in front of the TV rather than in front of each other. They can get out and away by car and plane. They can get a quick divorce. They can tune up the radio in order to tune out the family jangle. They can search out nonfamily peers for consolation by telephone. Like their eternity of ancestors, they can "busy" themselves as a form of escape. Unfortunately, none of these modern conveniences does one whit to cure the basic anguish. Even when they soothe superficially, they tend to exacerbate the ultimate pain of existence: the desperate sense of estrangement and loneliness.

That twentieth-century mortals have not found totally satisfactory answers to the tensions and hurts of intimacy is not surprising. Getting along with those closest to us is, and always has been, mankind's most basic behavioral conundrum. And yet the perversity persists that injuries to the psyche are sometimes prods to artistic creation and political leadership.

It is possible that the contemporary liberation for spouses and for the young, after the first disintegrating decades, may lead to a new maturity and a new commitment to the family community. The basis may be tactful leveling with one another, working at optimizing conflicting claims, finding activities that can be collectively pursued, recognizing the essentiality of spaces in togetherness, and rediscovering the magnificent psychic dividends of love and shared concern. Families of the future may find a new and enriching stability that can bless all the days of the extended decades of their lives. It is possible that the rediscovery and reconstitution of family relationships is the golden key—perhaps the only golden key—that ultimately can open the door to the larger world mankind seems to seek: individual freedom within the bounds of a friendly community.

The educational system has rich resources available to increase the individual's understanding of human psychology: systematic courses and modules in the behavioral sciences, philosophy, the fine arts, and religion; individual and group counseling; informative journals; and great literature in all of its forms—especially, perhaps, drama, poetry, prose fiction, biography, autobiography, and essays.

No part of the educational system is irrelevant in the purveying of psychological truths. In terms of alleviating the anxieties and containing the cruelties of human existence, no instrumental purpose has a higher priority.

The Search for Meaning

For centuries, the Judeo-Christian tradition brought to millions of people in the Western world a set of beliefs and principles that provided both a cosmic orientation and moral purpose. Even though many people still hold to the conceptual ikons of these theological traditions and an even larger number find intermittent solace and inspiration in the words and lives of sectarian prophets and saints, religious faith in late twentieth-century America is a waning phenomenon. Pounded out of shape by twentieth-century wars and depressions, dwarfed by the mind-boggling revelations of modern astrophysics, eroded by the realism and cynicism of contemporary philosophy, psychology, and literature, the Judeo-Christian tradition continues a long retreat that began with the Copernican revolution. That so many adherents remain is a tribute to the power of religious insight, imagery, and poetry to nourish and inform mankind's instinct for orientation.

It is the frustration of that instinct for orientation by cold drafts of agnosticism, atheism, and existentialist postulations of absurdity that marks the basic coping problem for many human beings in late twentieth-century America. If life is senseless on an aging planet in a meaningless and possibly dying universe, human fate is not tragic. It is not even absurd. It is simply, and in the most devastating psychological terms, inconsequential. That the pounding egos of the human race find it difficult to accept such a possibility is not strange. What is strange is that a scientific age should be so certain about the absence of meaning on the basis of such skimpy evidence. For, with all of the mythic character of traditional theology, it is surely conceivable that the religiously sensitive mind may be tapping a source and dimension of reality quite incapable of investigation by scientific empiricism and analytic reductionism. There are a sufficient number of friendly signs in existence (love, compassion, a sense of injustice, commitment to principle, beauty, art, music, the delights of intellectual discovery) to make the notion of complete absurdity itself completely absurd.

Furthermore, the inner peace that comes from disciplined meditation, the increasing evidence of thought transferences, the heightened probability of conscious existence in other galaxies and planetary systems, all raise at least the possibility that the universe is far friendlier than the "faithless coldness of the times" presently conveys. The search for a sense of belonging in man's universal home is not an inconsequential educational task. It is, on the contrary, an ultimate condition for reestablishing for vast numbers of people a sense of hope and purpose in life.

Generalized Problem Solving

One of the great fallacies of traditional schooling has been the assumption that knowledge, skills, and wisdom are all cut from the same pedagogic cloth. Too many people who acquire knowledge, in the sense of recognizing phenomena and calling them by name, may have no capacity whatever to apply such information or see its relationship to anything else. A person may know that swimming is manipulating arms and legs in such a way as to propel a person through water. He may even have seen slow-motion instructional films on swimming. But it is a far cry from the ingestion of this form of knowledge to actual and successful performance. Similarly, a knowledge of the possible consequences of behavior may not be enough to conjure gentleness in the face of acute provocation. As Elma Lewis has put it, "Most people [are] . . . just underdeveloped. You have to put a lot of work

in on yourself." James Coleman has called most
contemporary education for youth "knowledge-rich
and action-poor." It is probable that machine-graded
objective tests and the bland passivity of TV watching
and radio listening, as well as the attenuations of
adolescent dependency, have exacerbated the educational tendency to substitute a knowledge of isolated
impressions and facts for a working knowledge of
relationships, consequences, and skills. "Process," all
too often, has been an educational buzz-word without
kinetic or analytic implications for the learner.

To paraphrase the most fundamental of Dewey's
aphorisms, one learns to cope by coping, one learns
problem solving by solving problems. Effective and
efficient problem solving is, in many areas, specific
and is based upon the familiarities of repetitive con-
frontations. But beyond, there seems to be a generalized capacity for problem solving—a trained predis-
position, an inner confidence—that can substantially
facilitate a person's capacity for creative engagements
with obstacles and dilemmas of various kinds. In a
world disposed uncritically toward moral relativity,
one person's solution may, of course, be the essence
of another person's problem. Sensitive moral inquiry
leads to the conclusion that there are high-level as
well as low-level solutions to problems. There may
indeed be philosophical wisdom in the graffiti found
on a wall at Stanford University: "Pragmatism doesn't
work!"

But whatever the deeper philosophical problems
associated with educational purposes addressed to
increasing the individual's capacity to solve problems
there is prima facie evidence that the ability to demonstrate mastery of something is essential to a heightened
self-image, and that the confidence needed to attack
problems is inexorably tied to such a self-image. Such
evidence is presumably why David Riesman believes
that the educational system must insist that each child
demonstrate mastery of something (anything!) difficult. Demonstrated mastery is the precondition of that

degree of self-confidence needed for more generalized problem solving. Whatever the coping dilemmas of existence, the ultimate human freedom is the capacity to adjust the mind or adjust external reality to mitigate or transcend anxiety or pain. Surely a major instrumental purpose of education is, by appropriate exercises, to develop this capacity to the fullest. Up to now, our educational system has been slow in developing the inner confidence and the instrumental skills associated with a generalized capacity for problem solving.

Pedagogic techniques to achieve these ends are known. The encouragement of play and especially of fantasy among small children; informal apprenticeships allowing the young to work with parents or older siblings in finding the solution to home or travel problems; scholastic assignments and endeavors—curricular and extracurricular—that call upon the capacity of pupils for creative coping; for adolescents and adults, group leadership experiences such as those associated with Outward Bound. Almost all educational offerings can be given an activity twist. The success of computer-aided instruction and other forms of programmed learning is due in no small measure to the problem-solving frame of mind they stimulate in the learner.

Besides its patent utility, a generalized problem-solving capacity can pay impressive psychic dividends. Few psychic experiences can match the exuberant joy of what psychologists refer to as the "aha!" phenomenon—the inner delight of persons of all ages when they recognize that, as a result of persistent human observation and effort, a puzzle has been solved.

If all parts of the educational system should take seriously the instrumental purpose of increasing the individual's capacity to master the existential coping conundrums that surround him, the days would be brighter and the nights more restful for an overwhelming majority of human beings.

4

Work

O f the half-million hours of conscious existence, fewer than 90,000 hours—less than one-fifth of the total—will be spent "on the job," that is, working for paid remuneration. And unless there are substantial shifts in public policy, even these proportions will obtain for only two-thirds or less of the adult population between the ages of eighteen and sixty-five. The remainder will study, keep house, live on welfare, be unemployed, or be retired.

Yet most expectations of education are centered on preparation for work. The three Rs have been justified as the fundamental building blocks for future employability. Vocational education is a major and growing salient in both secondary and community college education. Since the founding of Harvard College in 1636, education for the professions has been a dominant purpose of colleges and universities. In recent years, a call for "career education" has infused the thinking of educational leaders at all levels. An increasing number of liberal arts colleges are placing special emphasis on their contribution to the future job-readiness of their students. Most parents continue to assume that whatever investment they make in the education of their children should pay dividends in the form of jobs; and, the more investment, the better should be the jobs for their offspring.

Furthermore, certain critics of higher education have raised the unsettling question of who needs college if most jobs can be performed by those without a college degree.

Unfortunately, the relationship of education to the world of work is fraught with conceptual and definitional problems. Quite apart from why less than 20 percent of the waking hours of most adults between ages twenty and eighty receive preeminent attention by educators, any discussion of education and work soon stumbles over issues of semantics. For example, are the words "job," "work," "career," "labor," and "employment" synonymous? Philosophers and social essayists have long exercised nice discriminations in this semantic jungle—and not without reason. When the question "Do you enjoy your work?" is followed by the answer (accompanied by a shrug) "Well, it's a *job*," most listeners sense that "work" and "job" are not synonymous. Thomas F. Green equates "job" roughly with paid employment, "labor" with spiritually unrewarding necessary activity whether paid or unpaid, and "work" with spiritually satisfying, purposive activity, paid or unpaid. In these terms, a person's "job" could be making commercial displays, his "labor" could be mowing the lawn, and his "work" could be landscape and portrait painting.

Even if one accepts the commonsense notion that education for work is education to prepare someone to earn a living, conceptual and definitional problems still abound. They are not resolved by the arbitrary categories employed by the Bureau of Labor Statistics. Is the work of a housewife "paid" or "unpaid"? When a farmer's twelve-year-old son works in the fields or the milking sheds and is fed and housed by his parents, is he "earning a living"? When a widowed mother is given Aid to Dependent Children allowances by the government, is she being "paid" for the "work" of raising youngsters, or is her deceased husband being indirectly and posthumously "paid" for work he did while he was alive? If someone trained as a professional engineer ends up driving a truck, is he "fully employed" even though "earning a living"?

These questions are not raised out of academic preciousness. Their answers have impressive consequences for those who decide that one of the major purposes of education is to prepare people for "work." But, first, some observations are in order about the present and probable realities of the American "job market," defined as the sum of persons in the society employed for pay or actively seeking such employment.

The Job Market

The irony in the present economic era is that, when educational purposes are being reduced in many minds to "training for jobs," the economy cannot provide enough jobs to absorb a substantial proportion of the people so trained. And at a time when higher education is still expected to prepare people for "interesting" jobs, the realization is growing that most jobs in a highly rationalized, division-of-labor technology are not, and probably cannot be made, vibrantly interesting to those who hold them.

When jobs are short, most people understandably concentrate their concern on the adult family breadwinner who loses his or her job. Catastrophic as unemployment may be in terms of status and self-image to the head of a family, he/she is not the only one to suffer in an economic system that largely shapes a person's definition of self according to occupational criteria. As women's rights become increasingly internalized as a social norm, housewives will suffer from the unavailability of paid jobs outside the house. If present trends continue, generations of young people will reach maturity with anywhere from 20 percent to 40 percent of their cohort unable to find paid jobs. In the mid-1970s unemployment rates for youth are almost three times the rate for adults. Among those who are both young and black or of Mexican, Puerto Rican, or American Indian descent, the rate of unem-

ployment exceeds 40 percent—six times the national
adult rate.

At the other end of the life cycle are uncounted
millions of older people who would take jobs if they
could find them. They have been relegated by social
and legal stereotypes and regulations to the ash can
of inutility. As the proportion of older people increases
and they live longer, as their health provides them
with additional margins of energy, and as inflation
continues, the pressures for rearranging remunerative
work opportunities to include the elderly may grow
exponentially.

Whatever the virtues of a mixed economy, a social
system that heaps "uselessness" on large segments
of young and old, and that subjects a substantial
proportion of adult breadwinners to ego scourges
according to the vagaries of economic cycles, that
system is surely an abomination.

Underemployment

But something more insidious seems to be emerging:
an economy in which the distress associated with high
unemployment is more than matched by "underemployment"—by a massive disenchantment with the
ego rewards of paid jobs that are dull, repetitive, and
spiritually unfulfilling. Close to 80 percent of all jobs
in the American economy can be learned in three weeks
or less by someone with a high school diploma. As
a larger and larger percentage of youth go on to some
form of postsecondary education, the risk of disenchantment with the existing world of jobs, even when
they are available, is likely to increase substantially.
The Bureau of Labor Statistics put it thus in their
1974 bulletin *Occupational Manpower and Training
Needs:* "Looking to the future, the question arises
as to whether the increasing educational attainment
of the population will continue to match the increase
in the number of jobs offering satisfactory employment
for those with higher education qualifications." But

the traumas involve more than those who will go on to postsecondary education. Why should high school graduates or even dropouts find spiritual satisfaction in occupations and labors rationalized for drones?

The educational implications of underemployment would be easier to identify if there existed a clearer set of data about job satisfaction in the United States. Most polls on job satisfaction over the past few decades have been remarkably consistent: most (70 to 80 percent) of those employed have indicated that they are either "satisfied" or "fairly well satisfied" with their jobs. Blacks, other minorities, and women rate their reactions considerably lower. A number of in-depth studies by psychologists and sociologists, on the other hand, reveal a widespread disenchantment with the impersonality, forced pace, routinization, and dead-endedness of many types of employment. Such disenchantment appears strongest among the young.

These divergent conclusions do not necessarily conflict. Respondents may well have layers of psychological response that are variously tapped by the casualness or the in-depth intensity of particular survey-research techniques. Interviewers may lead respondent reactions by the phrasing of questions or by subtle grimaces. Much may depend on the mood of those queried. For example, for many people there are moments when the routineness and repetitive character of employment is enormously consoling and reassuring, especially when contrasted with conjectures about unemployment on the one hand or anxiety-filled discretionary responsibilities on the other. (Foreman have five times the ulcer rate of their assembly-line workers.) On other occasions or at other levels of psychic probing, people may become (or be made) conscious of unfulfillments in their lives, including the lack of challenge and excitement in the way they earn their living.

There is a way of resolving the ambiguities in survey research results and case-study investigations. Two statements, one normative and one descriptive, have substantial validity. First, most jobs in the highly rationalized economy of America do not come close to tapping the full potential of the persons who occupy them. Second, since 1969, adults under age thirty, perhaps stimulated by the counter-culture of the 1960s, indicate job dissatisfaction in proportions significantly higher than do older age cohorts. Peter Berger touches the essential issue when he notes that society inculcates an expectation of meaningfulness in work—a promise of intrinsic reward and self-fulfillment. But most work situations cannot meet this expectation, and society does little to prepare its members for meaninglessness in their pursuits.

The logic of these realities for education depends on the nature of assumptions about the human condition, the malleability of state-supported capitalism, and the promise of competitive social systems. If the disutility of jobs is assumed to be man's fate, the educational system should patently use its good offices to prepare young people for the anguish of dull, painful pursuits. If, however, state-supported capitalism is viewed as the major culprit in depriving those employed of on-the-job "meaning," then education presumably should educate the present and potential leaders of the political economy to redesign the system, or, if that appears to be futile, to replace the system. But, if all conceivable competing social systems appear to be locked into a similar under-utilization of human potential in the world of paid work (and they appear to be), revolution (at least for this purpose) becomes meaningless, and we have come full circle to Adam's fall.

There is, however, a further issue. The external and internal props for translating the need to work into an economic growth work ethic have become weakened in the United States. The counter-culture, of course, rejects the very value premises of the work ethic. Hierarchical discipline in industry and commerce has been chastened by union power and by the human-relations-in-industry movements. The terrors of unemployment have been tempered by unemployment compensation, food stamps, and welfare payments. The intrinsic desirability of economic growth has been challenged by those who fear the consequence of wanton resource consumption. Status sensitivities and previous caste discriminations have caused whole ethnic and nationality populations to eschew certain types of menial but necessary jobs, or to put minimal energy in the performing of such jobs.

Cassandras in our midst claim that the consequences of all these things are clear: economic productivity as well as product and service quality will slump, inflation will become rampant in a slovenly society, the general standard of living will deteriorate, the slackening of psychic imperatives and externally defined standards will undermine individual and species potential.

The Challenge to Public Policy

This mine field of anomalies and somber possibilities cannot be wished away. Full employment—defined as jobs available for all those able and willing to work—is patently achievable. But until recently the conventional wisdom has been that a policy salient that moves even close to full employment will run afoul of rocketing inflation and punitive controls quite incompatible with the American tradition of personal and economic freedoms. Not only has this economic orthodoxy been challenged in recent years, but also the alternative extreme is grim indeed. For, if government does not work constructively on the policy problems of high unemployment, there is nothing in the history of capitalism to suggest that human resources will be fully and stably employed over long periods. This is true even if business were able to amass the investment capital it so desperately needs for sustained growth. And this analysis leaves out, of course, the possible effects of a vibrantly expanding economy on the quality and viability of the human environment.

Quite clearly a long continuation of high rates of unemployment among youth and the able aged is an explosive—and in the long run unacceptable—social and political condition.

Steering through the shoals of these and related dilemmas will be as serious a test of the creativity and resiliency of the American polity as can be imagined. It is probable that no single economic plan can be designed to overcome the economic paradoxes that envelop the nation (and the world). What can and must be done is to develop programs and procedures whose effect it will be to:

—increase the rate of job creation in both the private and the public sectors to the point where inflation and controls become unacceptable trade-offs; that point may well be far closer to true full employment than Cassandras believe;

—induce increased worker productivity as a buffer against inflation (to say nothing of state and local defaults and bankruptcies);

—provide for youth and for the able and interested elderly a combination of educational chances and public service job opportunities that can improve their sense of usefulness while helping to overcome the nation's tragic deficit of unmet social needs: urban blight, inadequate health care, sparse recreational facilities, crime, infant neglect, educational deprivation, environmental pollution.

On this final point, I believe that no more important investment in the future of this country can be conceived than making available to qualified unemployed and underemployed young and old, a series of teaching and tutoring opportunities, paid for in cash or in deferred educational fellowships. This arrangement would enable them to assist qualified professionals in improving the learning skills of the culturally and educationally deprived in our midst. Not the least benefit from such a policy would be that increased educational services are economic goods which do not pollute atmospheres or poison water.

Attitudes Toward Work

Is the availability of jobs enough? Is there not a need to begin to change the basic orientation of people toward the work segment of the existential wheel? Is not one of the instrumental purposes of education, using Professor Green's formulation, to enhance and extend the notion of the dignity of "work" and to help reduce to an irreducible minimum the indignity of "jobs" and the drudgery of "labor"? If so, then the educational system must direct people's attention to exploring alternative ways of approximating the conditions implicit in this formulation of instrumental purpose.

How, for example, can education help to destroy the invidiousness of distinctions that currently obtain among various forms and levels of purposive activity? Learning is work. Child rearing is work. Coping, transmuted from "labor" into a sense of mastery, is work. Some of the most satisfying aspects of the world of the free self involve work. The creative involvement of people in the form and substance of the enveloping polity is work. Purposive activity (either socially recognized or aesthetically satisfying to the individual) performed at levels of high standards of competence is for most people an enormously rewarding psychic experience. Pride in performance should therefore be a root instrumental purpose of education—an objective that is important to the successful carrying out of jobs, but that also supports and rewards all aspects of waking existence.

The way work performance is measured contributes to the tone and quality of a social order. American education has not set a good example. It has been encumbered with an enormous index of rank orders. Toward the top end of measured achievement or ability, whatever the motivational imperatives of the competition, the scramble is often vicious. Toward the bottom end, people can be disfigured, often for life, with the scar tissue of statistically determined "inferiority." To suggest that these offensive results of measurement can be entirely obviated by criteria-referenced examinations, or by changes in the structure of society, is to wish away one of the most intractable aspects of human experience. Results on criteria-referenced examinations are ego-satisfying until they become known by others. When known by others, comparisons—invidious or not—are virtually compulsive. And known results on criteria-based examinations can destroy a self-image at the same time that they rank-order competitors. Incidentally, communism does no better: the Soviet Union has one of the toughest competitive examination systems in the world; China rank-orders applicants for university admission according to their manifestations of Maoist loyalty, but it rank-orders nonetheless.

How to devise an educational strategy for increasing pride in performance without producing a dog-eat-dog competition among the able and hopelessness among the slow is a matter of continuing social priority. Despite all the difficulties and perversities noted above, it is still probable that recently devised criteria-based or competency-based examinations are friendlier to an elevated self-image for the majority than are traditional grading curves.

Basic Skills and Continuing Education

If enhancing the dignity of work is a major instrumental purpose of education, it is not the only purpose in this segment of the existential wheel. Surely, one major social justification for formal schooling is its training of the young in those basic skills of language and computation essential to gainful employment and other purposive activity. Those who emphasize mastery of the basic skills as *the* major instrumental purpose of education rest their case on the essentiality of the three Rs in virtually all aspects and functions of human life, most especially in earning a living. The most frequent complaint leveled by the economic community and by parents generally against the modern educational system is the alleged sagging performance in training young people to spell, to compute, to read, and to write with even minimal competency. The essentiality of these skills in the worlds of coping and of the free self is quite as impressive as is their relevance to the world of work. In many cases, their relevance to the world of work is secondary. Job-related motivations for mastering basic skills may be somewhat muted in a labor market where many of the available jobs are dull, dead end, and frequently undemanding. Needless to say, the more complex the jobs aspired to and the greater the hunger for future occupational and free-self options, the greater the need for basic-skill mastery.

To this point we have concentrated on attitudinal and basic-skill instrumental purposes of education vis-a-vis the world of work—especially among the young. There are a series of other work-related instrumental purposes of education that involve persons at various stages of development and a wide variety of agents and institutions in the total educational enterprise. One purpose is skill preparation for particular occupations and professions. Some of this education takes place in schools, colleges, universities, and proprietary educational enterprises. Much of it takes place through apprenticeships and other forms of inservice training. The best of this kind of education goes beyond narrow definitions of job skills and introduces students to larger issues of the relationships of the individual to machines, to peers, to supervision, to the organization as a whole, to consumers and clients. The truth is that the world of jobs, for most people,

involves a variety of relationships which, if properly
understood, can assist individuals in finding rewarding aspects of "work" in their "jobs" and their "labors."
One instrumental purpose of education then is to help
people find satisfaction in those personal relationships
that adhere to even the most repetitive and menial
of occupational functions. At more advanced levels,
especially in the learned professions, further learning
can help to update knowledge and skills in subject
areas that are rapidly changing. Continuing education
is especially important in view of the relicensing
regulations being imposed on selected professions by
state legislatures.

An additional instrumental purpose of the educational system, broadly conceived, is to prepare individuals for new jobs. Boredom, disenchantment, or
unemployment may prompt a person to seek out new
skills and new job opportunities. Facilitating this
process is important not only to the aspirants but also
to the society at large. For if preoccupation with
security, simple timidity, or lack of transitional "mid-
wives" lock unhappy people into their unrewarding
jobs, performance is bound to fall as morale sinks
or as the worker bumps the bottom of the psychic
pit.

In a previous chapter we touched on the need to
educate the older worker for retirement. This important
instrumental purpose of education merely needs underscoring at this point.

The Most Essential Instrumental Purposes

Basic skills training and continuing education,
important as they are, pale when compared to the
two most essential instrumental purposes of education
vis-a-vis the world of work: 1) to educate people to
see their lives as a whole, that is to see the world
of jobs in relationship to all other aspects of their
waking hours; and 2) to educate those who are in
a position to affect or exercise leadership (and that

includes most of us) to engineer or catalyze experiments in personalizing and deroutinizing the world of work.

As to the first, the projections of the life cycle indicate that most people will spend four to five times as many of their waking hours outside paid employment as in it. In this light, it is absurd to contend that education should focus largely on preparing young people for activities that will dominate only a quarter or a fifth of their conscious existence. And to make "gainful occupation" dictate social status and one's self-image is a dog-wagging operation of massive perversity and sullen consequence. Lest this view seems to undermine the struggle of women and minorities for occupational equality, let me add that jobs paid for in traditional ways will continue to be elements in people's calculations of personal and social esteem.

There is a related point of some importance. As income differentials among various kinds of jobs narrow, and as various kinds of payment including psychic rewards recompense people for their work as distinct from merely jobs, the worth of individuals will, it may be hoped, be computed increasingly on a nonoccupational basis. Since education is an integral part of salvation by works, why should not the term "unemployed" eventually be dropped from the lexicon of the American democracy except as applied to the few hopelessly lazy. The question "What do you do for a living?" could then be transmuted into "What do you do for a life?" "Where do you work?" into "Where do you function?" Such symbolic changes in our society will not come readily. But the claims of human dignity mandate educational efforts in these directions.

Meantime, much experimenting can be done to adjust the content, the context, and the scheduling of jobs with a view to narrowing the gap between "jobs" and "work" and to minimizing the ennui of "labor." Industry, here and abroad, has been experimenting with the reorganization of assembly-line functions, attempting to find "complete tasks" in which groups of workers participate in the rationalization of work assignments. Other industries and white-collar enterprises, public and private, are experimenting with flexible scheduling—allowing employees a choice about when during the day they wish to be on the job. Under this scheme, early risers might work from 7:00 a.m. until 3:00 p.m.; late risers from 10:00 a.m. to 6:00 p.m. Five hours of schedule overlap would allow for essential contacts. Still other firms and agencies are exploring a forty-hour, four-day week (four days of ten hours a day), thereby providing workers the flexibilities of a three-day weekend. Still other enterprises give workers incentives to move within the plant, to master a variety of jobs, to gain knowledge about, and a sense of identity with, the enterprise. Increasingly, employers of blue-collar and white-collar workers are providing inservice educational opportunities—partially or totally paid for by management—to enable employees to improve their chances for upward and lateral occupational mobility, to increase their general abilities, knowledge, and skills, or simply to break the lockstep of job monotony.

All of these ventures are attempts to find answers to a rising tide of dismay as people—especially young people—rebel against the dehumanizing aspects of employment in a highly bureaucratized and technological economic system. In spite of valiant experiments in rerationalizing job activities to make them conform more nearly to the claims for greater meaning, the movement is meager. Surely, an important instrumental educational purpose is to increase the attention of scholars, students, and practitioners to inadequacies in the world of work, with expectation of moving toward Kant's imperative that people be treated as ends not as means.

There may, of course, be limits to the rerationalization of jobs. Some work for all people, and much of it for most people, may continue to be drudgery. Acceptance of this possibility, building inner defenses against sullenness, taking pride in doing even menial jobs well, finding refreshment and opportunity for service to others in personal contacts and in on-the-job breaks, taking advantage of inservice training opportunities—these are directions to be studied and followed by those concerned with "career education." Job-related skills and attitudes of these kinds can shape morale, influence productivity, and condition rates of turnover. They can make or break an individual's inner sense of worth.

And, if it should be proven that most people are to be stuck most of their lives in jobs that are not substantially self-fulfilling, then the need increases dramatically for education to address the remaining segment of the existential wheel: the world of the free self.

5

The Free Self

"The pursuit of happiness" is one of the most enigmatic phrases in the Declaration of Independence. Is it a Jeffersonian literary conceit without substantive meaning? Is it a muddle-headed notion, happiness being, according to some, a by-product, not itself an object of pursuit? Or is it a phrase—singularly inspired—connoting a felicitous inner condition achieved by purposive activity? If the last is the case, and I believe it to be, such a condition is not likely to be realized through the passivities and diversions that characterize modern America.

The pursuit of happiness is an unending pilgrimage throughout conscious existence. Early chapters suggested that one can pursue happiness in work and in coping. Perhaps the ideal is that condition in which lines of demarcation dividing work, coping, and free self are obliterated, and each individual considers all activity as a maze of exploratory trails through which happiness may be pursued. However much can be done to reduce monotony and frustration in the worlds of work and coping, it remains that without a vibrant, energizing world of the free self, life will lack its most piquant flavor.

Historically most people have been so preoccupied and overburdened with labor and with coping that they have had little time for the world of the free self, for the part of the existential wheel that permits choice of experiences to delight or to satisfy the

voluntary sense of obligation. Even today, many people find themselves so laden with jobs, chores, health
problems, or family duties that they have little time
to cultivate the free self. The waking hours of the
mothers of young children, for example, are still
cluttered with coping. Compulsive persons, like the
shark that dies if it rests, pursue their frenetic tasks
from sunrise to midnight, acquiring money they will
never learn to spend for any enjoyment whatsoever.
But these are the exceptions.

Most Americans suffer not an absence of free time
but a serious incapacity to use a large amount of it
effectively. This opinion is, of course, a value judgment which can be dismissed as arrogant and elitist.
Who is to say that workers watching television at home
are less happy than rich patrons in the opera house?
Isolated invidious distinctions, however, are not the
issue. The issue is the pattern of activities (passivities?)
that constitute the world of the free self for most
Americans—the desensitizing and dehumanizing
character of the diversions that pummel us.

For decades Americans have been experiencing a
series of frightening escalations: an escalation of volume in the world of sound, of violence in life which
is reflected (and perhaps fomented) by the mass
media, of risk in sports spectaculars, and of hard
pornography in books, magazines, and movies. As
Saturday Review has pointed out editorially, the net
result of these neural onslaughts has been not only
an increase in violence and crime but also a massive
brutalization of our sensibilities. Entertainment based
solely on "kicks" leads ultimately to the encouragement of the demonic and the grotesque, to a
corrosive boredom for those who have seen or heard
everything. Dr. Estelle R. Ramey has called boredom
"the most prevalent American disease."

Furthermore, TV addiction and other recreational
passivities among the young appear to have other
untoward effects. They have been cited as possible

contributors to the startling decrease in both verbal and mathematical scholastic aptitude and achievement scores as measured by the major national testing agencies. Careful students of the influence of television on the American culture are beginning to identify even more unhappy consequences: a lessening of viewers' attention span; a debasing of social and cultural values to the extent that sensitivity to even violence and love are narcotized; a propensity to respond to the stimuli of the moment; a false sense of the possibilities of direct democracy, and a concomitant disenchantment with the political process (heavy TV viewers, according to Michael Robinson, are more apt to be turned off by politics than light viewers). These consequences have implications far beyond the free self, but they also mightily influence the nature and condition of the world of the free self.

If all of the violence, the speed, the noise, the sensations for kicks, the mindless options for new forms and intensities of stimuli, if they brought a heightened sense of joy—of inner satisfaction—to most people, they might be condoned. But psychologically they tend to leave people jangled and fretful. They create a frantic search for quick fixes to boredom and loneliness and end up stimulating both.

A projection of this klaxon ecology into the long future is as dispiriting a venture as the human mind can conjure. Alcohol and drugs then become the only salvation against the cold blasts of nothingness or the enervating stimuli of electronic prods.

Surely, the educational system has no higher function than to help people to have creative engagements with the world of the free self. For if the world of the free self is appropriately cultivated, its felicitous admixture of playfulness, concentration, and socializing can affect, infect, and help to liberate the worlds of work and coping. The free self then becomes not a mere segment of existence but a quality of existence.

The educational system knows far more about the

pursuit of happiness, about ways to enhance the world of the free self, than is generally understood. If our human inheritance is pondered carefully, it seems clear that lasting inner satisfaction comes from four sources: creating and appreciating beauty, enhancing physical satisfactions, performing obligations of service, and intensifying intellectual and emotional discovery. Education at its best is the key to each one of these worlds of satisfaction—of happiness.

Creating and Appreciating Beauty

One of the most reassuring of all human realities is the variety of aesthetic expressions and appreciations that reward the searching human spirit. One of the most sobering of all human realities is the complexity and the rarity of those preparations and contexts that permit truly rich and lasting aesthetic satisfaction. Education for creating and appreciating beauty is a highly complex endeavor. It is rarely treated as such, thereby leading to the inadequacy of most education that purports to increase the intensity and duration of aesthetic and sensual rewards.

One must begin, of course, with the extraordinary range of aesthetic preferences. Those who like Raphael rarely like Dali. Mozart-lovers often find electronic music baffling. Baroque architecture offends functionalists. Yeats and Pound wrote poetry for different ears. Lovers of Shaw may find Pinter an enigma. Gamemeat nauseates the tender-livered. Water skiers and fishermen find their spiritual refreshments in conflict. Hunters and bird-lovers have different definitions of joy.

One high function of education is to enrich aesthetic sympathies and tastes. This may not alter preferences, but it will extend perceptions, human understandings, and rewarding discourse.

Within any particular pattern of aesthetic preferences, however, education has a profound role in deepening an individual's understanding of the conditions of lasting satisfaction. Most Americans, for example, would echo Homer's lovely confession, "Dear to us ever is the banquet, and the harp, and the dance, and changes in raiment, and the warm bath, and love, and sleep." But even such elemental delights can be easily spoiled or their satisfactions minimized by variables of pace, of spacing, of degrees of satiation, of contextual discord. The point deserves elaboration.

If one judges by the historic themes and grace notes of poetry and prose, as well as by contemporary evidence, human beings find enormous aesthetic satisfactions in the elemental beauties of nature. Homer's "rosy-fingered dawn," the psalmist who lifted his "eyes unto the hills," Shakespeare's "bank where the wild thyme blows, "Wordsworth's "lonely as a cloud," Shelley's "blythe spirit," Yeats' "bee-loud glade," Masefield's "lonely sea and the sky"—these are poetic references that are familiar to the English-speaking world. But virtually every written and oral language in every epoch and on every inhabited piece of the earth's surface contains expressions of awe, wonder, and delight induced by the beauties of nature. I have been privileged in my work to travel widely. I already knew in exquisite detail what struck the spacemen so vividly from the vantage point of the moon: how incredibly beautiful the world is. I have seen pink on the glaciers of New Zealand's southern Alps; a blood red sun setting behind the dunes of the Libyan desert; the blue of the midnight moon on the snows of Kilimanjaro; a furtive mist edging the purple wilds of the Scottish moors; a montage of rocks, shells, and sea flowers in the tide pools of County Cork; the bounding swivel of an African impala; the defiant majesty of the Hindu Kush; Canada geese in all their mottled glory swimming their tidy file through the marshes of Kezar Lake in western Maine.

In each case, the aesthetic satisfaction was a function in no small measure of the solitude or the particular companionship that helped fix the context of the

appreciation. A dozen kinds of intrusions or dissonances would have, for me, curbed or destroyed the
ecstasy: a human quarrel, a loud radio, a noisy truck
or motor bike, a rifle shot, a factory pall of smoke,
a half-dozen discarded beer cans, raucous laughter,
a roadside advertisement, the smelly effluent of a paper
mill. On the other hand, time and again the beauty
could have been enhanced by greater knowledge:
historical associations; geological, astronomical, ocea-
nographic, and botanical nomenclature and principles;
apt literary and religious allusions from the recesses
of memory. I am convinced that dedicated and knowl-
edgeable bird watchers derive far more from forest
meanderings than I do. My wife, who is on a first-name
basis with trees and flowers, increases the sense of
belonging and the delights of discriminating perceptions of those who walk or ride with her. This is
not to say that natural beauty is satisfying only to
the learned. It is to say that the aesthetic satisfactions
related to natural beauty can be enhanced manyfold
by appropriate educational preparation.

What is true of the satisfactions of nature applies
equally to satisfactions in the arts. Most people spend
their lives oblivious to the intense, lasting satisfactions
of artistic expression. Most of us settle for fleeting
glimpses or halfhearted ventures into the world of
aesthetic adventure. And we are understandably put
off by those who feign knowledge of this treasure-filled
landscape in order to bolster their sagging egos or
their social status. Again, there is no need to denigrate
the untutored delights of most of us as we react to
commonplace aesthetic experiences: a pretty dress; a
haunting ballad; a good-looking car; a handsome
building; a pleasant flower arrangement; a beautifully
furnished room. Nor does it follow that unless one
really understands chamber music, opera, classical
ballet, abstract art, that one has not lived. No devices
measure intensities of satisfaction in aesthetic tastes
and preferences. The classical philosophical conun-

drum of whether beauty is objective or subjective is
still with us and is unlikely to be resolved. Some
art pleases precisely because it rolls over us like a
cool wave on a hot beach, because it massages or
stimulates noncognitive nerve ends. On the creative
side, some art pleases simply because it calls for little
effort: barbershop harmonizing; temple rubbings; cas-
ual picture taking.

Overall, however, those artistic experiences and
appreciations that leave a legacy of long-term satisfaction—whose delights linger and, in lingering, enrich
permanently—tend to be those that have been "worked
at," where literally "pains" have been taken: pains
of skill mastery, pains of discriminating thought, pains
of cultivated subtlety.

The essential fallacy in the more libertarian inter-
pretations of the counter-culture advice of the 1960s
to "let it all hang out" is that exposed flab is ugly.
Furthermore, extemporaneous, undisciplined expression is, within a short time, colossally boring. An
unrehearsed play, an untuned orchestra, a slapdash
finger painting, an unedited manuscript, a loose pile
of museum artifacts, an unchoreographed ballet—
these tend to attract limited interest because mind
has not been imposed upon emotion, arrangement,
or activity. All great art is an extraordinarily intellectual
exercise. On the creative side, it is the disciplined
manipulation of only semichoate blips emerging from
the unconscious self. On the receiving side, lasting
psychic fullness seems to be a direct function of the
active contribution—intellectual and emotional—
which witnesses and audiences are able to bring to
the aesthetic engagement. It is impossible to derive
substantial satisfaction from watching a Shakespearian
play if one is equipped with an English vocabulary
of, say, only 1,500 words, just as most of the beauty
of an Andrea del Sarto painting would be lost on
someone who is color blind. Ibsen's *Doll's House* has
special meaning for those engaged in the struggle for

women's liberation. The beauty of the Parthenon grows in the minds of those who have pondered aesthetic proportions or the cultural imperatives of fifth-century Athens.

To repeat: the world of the free self can be titillated but not fully and extensively rewarded by undisciplined or meagerly disciplined artistic creations and appreciations. Perversely, and a point too frequently forgotten by the pedants of humanistic learning, both artistic creativity and artistic appreciation can be "sicklied o'er" if the "pale cast of thought" is too elaborate, too mechanical, too patterned. Some canons of rationality have to be temporarily suspended if the mind's holy-of-holies is either to produce or to receive artistic enlightenment. Generations of insensitive literature teachers have parsed the euphony out of Shakespeare for tens of thousands of bored and thus deprived students. If consciousness of symphonic structure is too insistent, the tonal gestalt evaporates.

But most aesthetic deprivation is due to lack of education rather than to miseducation. As for music, an additional enemy of aesthetic satisfaction has been the deafening decibels of electronic amplification and the ubiquity of radio, tapes, and discs in public places. The cheapening of music through oversupply and overpowering volume seems to me one of the saddest of today's realities. What is surely one of the most magnificent of life's experiences has been made available to hundreds of millions of human beings by the inexpensive wizardry of modern communications technology. But the process has been so indiscriminate that much of music's savor has been concomitantly removed. Young people have compensated, in part, by investing heavily in superb stereophonic sound equipment for home enjoyment. But in its most elaborate manifestations, this delight is available only to the rich.

How to offer instruction in the disciplines and the emotional conditions conducive to personal enrichment through the arts is, or should be, a matter of highest educational priority. Whatever sense of national community is promoted by network sports and newscasts, we are being all but deadened aesthetically by the violence and inanities of most TV programing. Too often, education in the arts is considered a frill that can be discarded when budgets are tight. The shortsightedness of this value decision is appalling. If K-12 is forced to disown responsibility in this essential area, colleges and universities and cultural resources in the larger community must provide corrective and compensating instruction. And government and voluntary financial support for the Public Broadcasting Service must be sustained and increased.

Enhancing the Satisfaction of Physical Activity

If the creation and appreciation of beauty is an endless frontier in the world of the free self, it is not the only area of personal adventure. The cultivation of bodily skills and conditions is another area of extraordinary satisfaction. I have mentioned the importance of diet and exercise in promoting longevity and health. But beyond the therapeutic advantages of bodily care, physical competencies and their concommitant sense of well-being are associated with some of life's most delightful and sustaining experiences. A moment's reflection will underscore this truism. Who will forget the exhilaration of not losing one's balance in hop-scotch, balancing a bike, learning to dance, perfecting a second serve, hitting a stick ball, staying out of the gutter in bowling, learning to follow through in a golf drive, being able to negotiate a slalom course, making three out of four free-throws in basketball, or of cutting to the right as well as to the left in ice hockey?

One of my favorite people in the world has derived great satisfaction over the years from teaching people how to swim. The development of this skill brings not only the satisfaction of grace in movement and stamina in performance, it brings with it an enormous release from anxiety. Few behavioral changes are more marked, or more intrinsically satisfying to both student and instructor, than the transformation of a timid, spluttering, awkward, helpless thrasher into a confident, graceful, and versatile swimmer. And swimming opens up a whole range of other aquatic sports—water-skiing, sailing, boating, fishing, surfing—which otherwise would also be anxiety-ridden.

For many people, great and lasting satisfactions come from the preparation and consumption of food. If cooking and serving a meal are viewed as creative challenges that bring delight to oneself and to others, the resentment often associated with this aspect of coping is transmuted into a happy engagement. Similarly, the cultivation of taste in food and drink can be a rewarding experience and a matter of lifelong satisfaction. Again, all of this takes "working at" and can be facilitated by appropriate instruction. Of course, all the instruction does not have to take place in formal classrooms: TV, radio, tapes, platters, discs, informal adult education programs, and self-instruction through reading can all make substantial contributions.

Since the world of periodicals and books has become surfeited with instructions on perfecting sexual techniques, nothing needs to be noted here except for underlining the physical and psychic delights of contextually appropriate sexual relationships. Education is most profoundly relevant to sexual fulfillment if it reminds us (to paraphrase Matthew Arnold) that the spirit we are of and the context we create is infinitely more important than the techniques we employ.

Mastery over the machines and artifacts of technology and the vagaries of nature is another avenue to satisfaction in the world of the free self. For millions of people, knowledge of "how to make it," "how to fix it," or "how to grow it" is a key to psychic completeness. The process may involve skill with a sewing machine, a mechanical saw, a drill, a hammer, a cultivator. It may involve a knowledge of circuits, solenoids, carburetors, tensile strengths, fertilizers. It may encompass dexterity with needle and thread, a potter's wheel, a plumber's snake, a trowel. But once again, "make it," "fix it," or "grow it" skills can bring lasting satisfaction to the world of the free self; they can bring free-self skills and attitudes to bear in the worlds of work and coping. Both formal and informal educative instruments and agencies can help to extend capacities and skills in these ubiquitous preoccupations of modern life.

Patently, all concern with physical activity does not have to be—must not be—purposive exertion. Lazing or hacking about, watching sports live or on TV, laughing at inanities, playing cards with friends, engaging in festivals—in limited doses these are as important to the free self as a fallow field is to growing crops.

Performing Obligations of Service

It may seem strange to the modern mind to be reminded of concepts like "obligation" and "service" which, however rich in their religious and ethical ancestry, seem to have lost much of their motive force after the end of the Victorian era. Perhaps their fall from grace was a consequence of the static savagery and unrelieved filth of trench warfare in World War I. Millions of young people on both sides entered that extended conflict with a powerful sense of obligation. "The Service" in those days meant military employment and deployment. The shattering of idealism, so stunningly depicted in Paul Fussell's *The Great War and Modern Memory,* has been one of the overwhelming realities of modern existence.

And yet, even with the twentieth-century's massive depreciation of Victorian rhetoric, millions of people have continued to find nourishment for the free self in fulfilling perceived obligations and in performing voluntary services. I remember my father donning his greatcoat on a blustery night of snow and wind preparing for a mile walk and saying, "I do not *want* to go to the meeting of the prudential committee of the church, but I *ought* to go!" Upon returning, he would smile and say simply, "Well, I have done my duty."

Some years ago during an active political life in Middletown, Connecticut, I came to know hundreds of people who found meaning and satisfaction in performing community services: volunteer firemen, members of library boards, organizers of community chests and United Fund drives, hospital aides, readers for the blind. These activities were frequently in addition to service on PTA committees or church boards and participation in service-club benefits for the crippled. There is no way of measuring growth or reduction in this kind of activity. The welfare state, fear of the streets, the lazy seduction by TV have probably eroded the frequency and degree of the service commitment. A substantial amount still remains, including that of young people, and the opportunities for effective service to others are almost limitless. Schools and colleges, churches and synagogues, service clubs and media give conscious attention to identifying service opportunities. These brokerage functions could become more effective if they emphasized the importance of volunteer service in the satisfaction both to the volunteers and to those directly served.

Attention will turn in the next chapter to the relationship of education to the formal polity. But no reform of the bureaucratic and political system can possibly obviate the need for the intimate expressions of caring that are associated with the voluntary performance of works of obligation and service. Most of our formal educational instruments give inadequate attention to the psychic fulfillments that derive from doing one's duty and from serving one's fellow human beings in a spirit of consideration and friendliness.

The Satisfactions of Intellectual and Emotional Discovery

If appropriately exercised, the most durable and satisfying organ of the human body is the brain. Just how mental processes function is still a mystery. The mind is its own greatest frontier. Some patterns of thought, of course, are psychologically destructive. Yet few human experiences can match in sheer exhilaration the rewards of the cultivated human mind at play and at work along the frontiers of its capacity. Such work and play are often justified and financed on the grounds that they will help to solve national and international problems. And so they will. But disciplined and creative intellectual activity is also an end in itself.

Reflecting upon his seven decades of life, E. B. White has said, "I cherish the rememberance of the beauty I have seen. I cherish the grave, compulsive word." That "beauty" and "the grave, compulsive word" should occur in tandem in one of twentieth-century America's most truly cultivated minds is surely no accident. The distance between human beings and other primates is most significantly marked by communication. Words are the brain's instruments of internal dialogue, of relating ideas to others, of taming objects and events to a point conducive to manipulation, and of resisting manipulation by others. Words are the rhetorical weapons of peaceful conflict resolution. They are carriers as well as befuddlers of rationality.

Above all, they are the key tools of discovery—intellectual and emotional. In a world where physical frontiers now need exploitation only to the point of carefully considered conservation, and space frontiers involve high technology and the advanced professional competence of a few, the lasting delights of discovery for most people must be along the frontiers of the mind. For natural scientists, working and playing along this frontier calls for a huge array of the instruments of refined empiricism. For many social scientists and humanists, a knowledge of the modern paraphernalia of symbolic logic (and its limitations) is essential to rewarding discovery. But for most people, intellectual adventure is the experience of crossing clearings made by others. Such is the fascination of watching Jacques Cousteau on television or a play of Sophocles on the stage. It is especially the fascination of reading the "grave, compulsive word" wherever it, in combination, appears in an intellectually challenging and aesthetically satisfying way.

Reading is essential to most occupations and to most successful coping. It is the key to understanding and improving the enveloping polity. But it is also the most liberating of all the instruments that affect the world of the free self. The impoverishment of many souls is a direct function of their inability or unwillingness to read.

The rewards to the free self of reading are multifaceted. Some reading is largely undemanding and is undertaken for pure relaxation and delight: A. A. Milne, P. G. Wodehouse, Agatha Christie—the reader's list is as good as mine. Here, the rewards of "discovery" come from a felicitous turn of either phrase or events. Some reading is simply a pursuit of knowledge and demands attention on the part of the reader and clarity on the part of the author. Great reading, however, is a search for wisdom through interaction with ideas compellingly expressed on the printed page. Great reading makes one's own internal dialogue three-dimensional. It creates explosions of insights and sunbursts of aesthetic pleasure. It can be suited to mood. Of all human activity, it is the one most congenial to satisfying people's instinct for orientation—their desire to know who they are, where they have come from, their destiny. If there are no final answers, human beings have infinitely more understanding of the mythic images that line the walls of Plato's cave than did their distant ancestors. And they know the psychological nourishment which that strange combination of peace and excitement called revelation can bring to the troubled mind. What tends to distinguish revelation through reading and revelation through evangelical preaching is that reading permits running and repeated criticism. The mind can tinker with the heart and give it the steadying therapy of continuing reflection.

For those who have never been induced to enter the written world of comparative religion, moral philosophy, cross-cultural literature, or intellectual history, this recitation may seem irrelevant and pretentious. The mood of our present age is both antihistorical and antiprophetic. But as Harvey Cox has pointed out, "Cut a man off from his memories or his visions and he sinks into a depressed state. The same is true for a civilization. . . . When a civilization becomes alienated from its past and cynical about its future, as Rome once did, its spiritual energy flags. It stumbles and declines."

Cox's view suggests that a major key to reversing the alienation and the cynicism of the modern era is to rediscover the past and to postulate futures that are both reasonable and desirable. Both the past and the intellectual stimulation for the future live predominantly and supremely in our libraries. Perhaps the most exalted responsibility of professors and of literary critics is to guide people to those books and articles that will help them in the world of their free selves to discover or rediscover who they are and what they have the chance of becoming.

The literary and philosophical mood of the twentieth century has been understandably pessimistic. The smugness of the Victorian era, uncritical projections of the eighteenth-century faith in progress, the idea that the conquest of nature and the fulfillment of universal democracy were just around the corner—all these moods and notions have been dashed against twentieth-century realities of wars, depressions, and Frankenstein technologies.

This disillusionment gives a special urgency to restoring man's sense of his own nobility—"man" used of course in its generic sense. The insistent message of the prophetic geniuses of history is that there is a qualitative difference between man and beast—that man has the capacity to enter into a special relationship with the universe and that this special relationship is man's glory and meaning. The Psalmist asked the appropriate question and affirmed the appropriate answer:

> When I consider Thy heavens, the work of Thy fingers, the moon and the stars which Thou hast ordained, what is man that Thou art mindful of him, and the son of man that Thou visitest him? For Thou has made him a little lower than the angels, and has crowned him with glory and honor.

We, in this century, need no blind poet to remind us of our Paradise Lost, nor a William Blake to illuminate the convolutions of hell. We in this cataclysmic epoch know how far man has fallen. But to fall is one thing; to despair is quite another. We despair, and we have forgotten why we despair. Fundamentally, we despair not because of external horrors or existential suspicions of personal mortality. We despair because we have forgotten our place in the universe, because we have become so preoccupied with man as animal and man as object that we have forgotten man as creative spirit and man as noble subject. In the name of realism we have fashioned a monstrous caricature. We have accepted Jonathan Swift's view of man as 'Yahoo,' while ignoring the nobility which Swift transferred satirically to the horse but which can be discovered only in the heart and mind of man.

Why do we forget so easily? What has happened to us in this generation that we ignore the capacities and promise of man? We study the ashes and ignore the phoenix. We dwell upon our failings and shrug off our triumphs. We see London through the eyes of Hogarth and pretend that Christopher Wren never lived. We have become aliens in our universal home because we have become aliens to ourselves. We are storm-weary. The turbulence of violent change in this century has plunged us—like a frail aircraft—into a towering cloud of spiritual darkness from which no escape seems possible. The difficulty is that history's lessons are so frequently forgotten or ignored—the transient nature of all thunderheads no matter how massive, and the buoyancy of the wings of the human spirit for negotiating attenuated stress. In disproving progress we have forgotten the reality of the Pilgrim's Progress. Writing in the dingy jail of Bedford, John Bunyan, in his great allegory, lets Christian fall into the clutches of Giant Despair. Giant Despair's castle (which Bunyan astutely labels Doubting Castle) has a black dungeon with no possibility of escape. But finally the prisoner plucks from his own bosom a key called Promise and opens wide the dungeon door into a larger life.

Every educational institution is in part a Doubting Castle—for one of an education's prime responsibilities is to doubt. But the other great responsibility of education is to affirm, to establish fertile hypotheses about the nature of man.

Surely this is the supreme contribution of educators to their students and to each other: to rekindle excitement in life by touching the fire of man's promise to the wick of learning. Far too often we have settled for less. We dissect man. We put calipers upon his littleness. We mechanize and quantify him. We spell out with excruciating candor his palpable failures of nerve and intelligence and benevolence—individually and collectively. We thrust our telescopes into the blackness of infinity, and poke our cameras into the fitful trackings of subnuclear activity; and we ignore the wonder of what we observe and the even greater wonder of the observer's eye and mind. We measure IQs and dismiss as irrelevant the quotients of beauty and goodness.

The ultimate business of education is human freedom. If human freedom means nothing but the sad and sorry flow of existence upon a well-documented darkling plain, the charge to graduates should be to push the button when they have the chance. If the human race has in fact been caught up in an irreversible ebb tide, if Matthew Arnold's transient mood at Dover Beach has become an eternal condition, then it is irrelevant whether the missiles fall. For the option is an endless melancholy, a sullen ennui—deaf to the song of the thrush, blind to the evening sky, and indifferent to the creative wonders of man's mind and hand.

If new purpose, new adventure, new excitement in living are to emerge for most people in their jobs and in their coping—if work is to be enhanced and coping is to be subject to increased mastery—it will happen in part because of spill-overs from an enriched world of the free self. But even these gains will be muted unless attempts are made to make the enveloping polity friendlier than it now is to the stages of individual development and to all three conscious segments of the existential wheel.

6

The Enveloping Polity

The American polity may be characterized as a system of state-supported capitalism, political and bureaucratic federalism, and constitutionally protected criticism.

Global and domestic economic, political, and social forces are placing unprecedented strains upon this system.

These twin propositions might simply be filed as written were it not that, currently and prospectively, they impinge massively on the existential realities described in previous chapters. Life begins and ends as a vital statistic of government. National security and diplomatic operations are justified as protectors of life and liberty. Publics invest in state-supported schools in the belief that schools have the capacity to contribute substantially to the cognitive and affective development of young people. Laws governing child labor affect the trauma of adolescence. Social security and Medicare substantially influence the conditions of old age. All segments of the existential wheel are shaped and affected by the laws, institutions, and behaviors of the political economy: the availability and quality of jobs and the distribution of wealth outside the job market; the coping agenda, including coping with taxes and with myriad public regulations; the external supports to the free self, including the availability of educational, cultural, and recreational resources and facilities; and definitions of freedom permitting the exercise of individual options.

The American commonwealth is far too complex for rational control at the center—at least without the use of punitive government sanctions quite out of keeping with our peacetime national heritage. The result is a bizarre kaleidoscope of centers of political and economic power. Some of these centers are public, some private, some mixed. They exist at all levels of constitutional federalism: national, state, and local. In the eyes of devotees, the American polity provides most citizens with freedom and security and with a high standard of living. In the eyes of its critics, it promotes real freedom and exorbitant wealth for a few at the price of massive caste and class inequities, demeaning bureaucratic strictures and regulations, militarism, and a cultural crassness that dehumanizes its citizens.

The fundamental conundrum is how to overcome the evils postulated by critics without destroying the virtues claimed by devotees. For rigid ideologues of the right and the left, of course, no answer is possible. "Free enterprise" reactionaries, consciously or unconsciously using Darwinian analogues, argue that inequality is a law of nature. Social as well as individual wealth, they assert, is the product of decisions by Prometheans motivated by the possibilities of material gain. The appropriate job of government then is minimal: to establish the framework within which a free-market economy can prosper, and to handle social and economic basket cases among the unfortunate. Critics to the left, on the other hand, believe that a free market is an illusion, that state-supported capitalism is inherently exploitative, protective of the rich, and dangerously militaristic; and that either a strong central authority organized to plan for economic justice, conservation, and peace, or a political economy divided into pastoral communes is the way to salvation.

Most Americans appear to disavow ideological extremes. To paraphrase Justice Holmes, they have little faith in utopias and almost none in sudden ruin. They hope to find a middle way that optimizes a number of competing values: options for the individual, a redress of the intolerable grievances of caste and class, a diplomatic and military posture consistent with a progressively ordered and equitable global network of nations and peoples, and a stable economy friendly to the ecology of the biosphere. They believe governments are needed as major instruments in a search for optimized trade-offs. They also believe, however, that governments are part of the problem as well as part of the solution. They know that statesmen can corrupt and can be corrupted. They know that, at some point, the apparatus of government monitoring and regulation becomes a cure worse than the disease being attacked. They have a vague sense that individual citizens have a responsibility to participate in the political processes. Beyond voting, letters to editors and politicians, and street protests, however, they are not clear how participation can or should be exercised.

The test of the viability of some middle way, some "vital center," has never been more severe. If the phrases in the Preamble to the Constitution are employed as bench marks for measuring the adequacy of our political economy, the shortfalls are patent.

A More Perfect Union? There are ominous signs that America is being retribalized into ethnic, religious, racial, economic, demographic, and sexual divisions. White suburbs surround black and brown inner cities. Zoning ordinances keep the riffraff out. Generations talk with each other fitfully across moats of misunderstanding. Self-interest and self-indulgence flout the very notion of community.

Establish Justice? America, in an orgy of litigiousness, has overcrowded its court dockets, pampered rich litigants, frustrated the poor and the middle class, and produced more lawyers than is compatible with a nation built on unspoken assumptions of mutual trust.

Insure Domestic Tranquility? The headlines of

crime and violence and the ubiquitous ads for personal
and home security devices tell the sad tale of where
we are.

Provide for the Common Defense? In spite of moun-
tains of riches spent on armaments, America is part
of an international disorder that is almost bound to
confront humankind with a continuation of international kidnapings, violence, and terrorism; a series
of small flames of belligerency in a forest of tinder;
planetary economic bargainings that America may not
win; and an escalating risk of nuclear piracy and
blackmail.

Promote the General Welfare? This entire essay is
directed at the disturbingly uneven state of the general
welfare—psychological, economic, social, and political.

Secure the Blessings of Liberty? Here, quibbles
aside, the United States on any scale of nations is
still in the front rank of societies that enjoy political
freedom. The question is whether the parlous state
of the nation in other respects will erode and destroy
this cardinal condition of its self-renewal. Fear is the
most brutalizing of human emotions. If social path-
ologies—for example, crime, unemployment, racial
conflicts, international tension—become sufficiently
unsettling as to produce widespread personal fear,
people will trade freedom for security by electing
despots. So runs one of the oldest principles of political
action. This truth is so basic that it deserves elaboration.

Ancient Lore on the Conditions of Freedom

The ancient chronicles of mankind are freighted
with examples of domestic turbulence. The historian
Thucydides believed that domestic turbulence was
inevitable. To him it was simply the overt manifesta-
tion of the cycles of history kept revolving by what
he called "excess of power." According to Thucydides,

"primitive despots start the wheel rolling. The more power they get the more they want, and they go on abusing the authority until inevitably opposition is aroused and a few men, strong enough when they unite, seize the rule for themselves. These, too, can never be satisfied. They encroach upon the rights of others until they are opposed in their turn. The people are aroused against them, and democracy succeeds to oligarchy. But then again the evil in all power is no less operative. Democracy brings corruption and contempt for law until the state can no longer function and falls easily before a strong man who promises to restore order. The rule of the one, of the few, of the many, each is destroyed in turn because there is in them all an unvarying evil—the greed for power—and no moral quality is necessarily bound up with any of them."

Plato and Aristotle subscribed to elements of Thucydides' cyclical theme of history. For them the two great political evils were libertarian democracy and dictatorship, and they believed that the first led inexorably to the second. Plato, for example, devotes the entire third book of his *Laws* to an examination of the opposites, to Persian tyrant kings, and to how an unrestrained democracy in Athens ruined itself by an excess of liberty. Plato's *Laws* are to me far more rewarding than his *Republic*. The latter is totalitarianism idealized. The *Laws,* on the other hand, deals with real people in a real world. The good or approximately good society to which the third book of the *Laws* is addressed, is a society which maximizes law-abiding rule—which features, in other words, domestic tranquility. For as Plato and as Plato's pupil, Aristotle, contended: in any good state, the law must be the ultimate sovereign and not any person whatsoever. They perceived a universal moral precept: that constitutional rule is consistent with the dignity of the subject, whereas personal or despotic rule is not.

What, then, undermines the rule of law? What causes

domestic strife and political decay? Was Thucydides right that greed for power is the basic cause of civil unrest? Most political theory addressed to this question from ancient to modern times has identified a second causative factor: inequality.

Plato fully believed that, at least in Greek experience, excessive differences between rich and poor had been the chief cause of civic contention. Aristotle believed that revolutions are caused chiefly by inequalities in property, a theme later to be elaborated by many other political theorists, including Karl Marx.

Sir Thomas More, in his biting sixteenth-century satire *Utopia,* points out that crime in England is alarmingly common but that, in a grotesquely unequal society, crime is the only livelihood open to a great number of persons. In as terrible a voice as his pen can conjure, More fairly shouts at the England of his day, "What other thing do you do than make thieves and then punish them?"

In the nineteenth century, in the quieter vein of a Victorian Oxford don, T. H. Green writes, "It is idle to expect men to become responsible agents when they live in conditions that destroy the qualities of character on which responsibility depends."

When inequality and power-hunger remain uncorrected by government and by private virtue, the basic corruption of the political order ensues. Machiavelli, in the sixteenth century, describes political corruption as including "all sorts of license and violence, great inequalities of wealth and power, the destruction of peace and justice, the growth of disorderly ambition, disunion, lawlessness, dishonesty, and contempt for religion." And according to Machiavelli, when the necessary virtues have decayed, there is no possibility of restoring them or of carrying on orderly government without them except by despotic power. And despotic power is infinitely preferable to anarchy.

This last theme appears in stirring eloquence in the writing of Thomas Hobbes more than a century

later. In his great work *The Leviathan,* Hobbes conjec-
tured that man is basically selfish and power seeking,
that the rewards of nature are in short supply, and
that, in the competition for the scarce goods of life,
there would be a "war of every man against every
man" if it were not for a contrivance called government.
Without government, life would be [perhaps Hobbes's
most famous phrase] "solitary, poor, nasty, brutish,
and short."

If power-hunger and inequality constitute the main
threats to domestic tranquility, what then are the
conditions of domestic stability? Obviously, the answers are: 1) reduce inequality and 2) set up agreed-
upon rules including checks and balances to ensure
that power is contained and that alternations of power
are peaceable rather than disruptive.

On reducing inequality, Plato wanted to limit the
amount of property that anyone could hold in order
to "exclude from the state those excessive differences
between rich and poor which Greek experience has
shown to be the chief cause of civic contention."

Aristotle believed that equality (and consequently
domestic tranquility) was synonymous with a large
middle class—neither very rich nor very poor. As
Euripides had said years before, the middle class is
the class that "saves states." Politically, Aristotle
thought that a combination of oligarchy and democracy
was the most stable form of government. If not watched
by the people, the oligarchs—or privileged few—
would become oppressive, and this oppressiveness
would breed disorder. Without the balance wheel of
the privileged few, the democratic masses would be
rudderless, and the ship of state would founder.

Echoes of the Greek philosophers' twin ideas of
mixed and balanced government and greater equality
can be heard throughout the succeeding centuries—up
to and including our own. Certainly these are the
golden themes of our Founding Fathers: the equality
doctrine especially noted in our Declaration of

Independence; the mixed and balanced government concept in our Constitution.

The essential legacy of the theory of mixed and balanced government and of greater equality must constitute the bedrock of American citizenship education. The lessons are clear: there is no possibility of domestic tranquility in a free society without a progressive increase in social justice; if sufficient power is to be aggregated to make effective government possible, both institutional and political means must be found to hold such power accountable. In these terms, the realities of our racial and economic castes and classes explain a sizable proportion of our lack of domestic tranquility. The trauma of Watergate is a reminder of the need to hold power accountable.

Participation and Representation

Fundamental to the success of a free society is widespread citizen participation in the political process. This participation may include voting; party and interest-group activities; performing such public functions as jury duty, testifying as a witness, and serving on public boards and commissions; and carrying out honorably the mandates of obeying laws and paying taxes. Beyond this, citizens contribute to the polity by keeping informed about public affairs and by sharing their views with other citizens and with elected representatives. An independent press and a rich smörgasbord of information purveyed by TV, radio, journals of opinion, and books, are essential to the maintenance of a politically literate society.

Much of the real power of citizens, however, is latent. It lies in the perpetual threat to politicians of retribution at the polls if citizens, otherwise passive, are outraged by the direction or corruption of public life. Former Harvard professor Carl Friedrich once called this "the law of anticipated reaction." It is a moralizing force of incalculable significance to the workings of democracy.

For reasons that are understandable in the sociology of reform, the air is filled with romantic half-truths about the possibilities and desirability of extending and increasing direct citizen participation beyond the activities and latencies just listed. Because the nation has recently been burned by abuses of power, some high-minded reformers and concerned educators have developed ("refurbished" is a better word) a democratic litany as superficially plausible as it is operationally specious and even dangerous. Two propositions seem to dominate: first, citizens should wherever possible participate directly in all political decision making; second, where they cannot participate directly, the decision processes of their representatives must be open to detailed and continuous public monitoring. Following in the footsteps of the reform movements at the turn of the century—especially the tarnished movements for the initiative, referendum, and recall— modern reformers seem to have little understanding of the complexity of the agenda of modern government, of the interest-group building blocks of public policy, and of the essential conditions of aggregating and exercising responsible political power. In consequence, they establish reform paradigms that are frequently irrelevant, naive, or mischievous.

For those reformers who believe in universal, direct citizen participation in public affairs, whose model democracy is the New England town meeting (which, incidentally, usually was and is caucus-rigged), technology is surely available. The government could, at modest expense, equip every TV set in the nation with "yes" and "no" buttons. Every Sunday night at 8:00 p.m., three national, three state, and three local propositions could be flashed on the screen. The citizen would simply vote yes or no. On the first trial Sunday, the propositions, for example, might be as follows:

National
  Proposition One: The Federal Reserve rediscount rate should be lowered by a quarter of a point. Yes ___ No ___

Proposition Two: Five nuclear submarines should be built instead of two aircraft carriers. Yes ____ No ____

Proposition Three: Gold should be remonetized for purposes of stabilizing international currencies. Yes ____ No ____

State

Proposition One: State environmental protection laws should limit sulphur emissions of factories to one particle in 10,000. Yes ____ No ____

Proposition Two: Offender farms are 25% less secure than traditional prisons, but their rate of recidivism is 25% less. Should the state substitute the farm system for the prison system? Yes ____ No ____

Proposition Three: The state budget should shift from a line-item to a program-budget format. Yes ____ No ____

Local

Proposition One: School bonds should be marketed only if the interest rate is under 10%: Yes ____ No ____

Proposition Two: Most recent hirings of municipal employees have been minorities and women. Now that retrenchment is necessary, seniority should still determine who is to be laid off first. Yes ____ No ____

Proposition Three: The local police department should be amalgamated with the new metropolitan police system. Yes ____ No ____

Even if a packet of printed materials were delivered well in advance, or a two-page spread of editorial comment appeared in the Sunday newspaper, how reasonable is it to assume that most citizens would have the information or would take the time to master the data and to make analyses sufficient for informed judgments? Frequently, propositions placed on the ballot under various referendum provisions are decided on the basis, not of study, but of simplistic reactions to PR techniques or to calls for party or interest-group loyalty.

Because I have great faith in the ultimate capacity of American citizens to make wise, fundamental value choices, I lament attempts to induce them into making superficial technical choices. Representative legisla-

tors and officials supported by an educated bureauc-
racy, informed by myriad interest groups and experts,
checked by an independent judiciary and a free press,
and held accountable to the larger public through
periodic elections, intermittent correspondence, and
occasional face-to-face meetings—all this constitutes
not only a reasonable apparatus for conducting modern
public business in an economically and technologically complex free society like the United States,
but also it is the *only* reasonable apparatus.

But there are necessary conditions if this complex
apparatus is to work effectively. One condition is that
politicians and media must really work at reducing
technical questions to the level of value choices that
are in fact amenable to public discourse and to ultimate
resolution at the polls through expressions of preference for persons and parties. A second condition is
that opportunities be provided for interest-group
inputs into the decisional processes of government,
but not for minority-based vetoes of the actions of
legitimate majorities and authorities. This last point
needs emphasis. James Madison, in the tenth Federal-
ist Paper, wrote of the inevitability of interests and
factions in a free society. He contended that the
regulation of these various and interfering interests
forms the principal task of modern legislation (emphasis supplied). Madison's choice of *regulation* instead
of *accommodation* implies authority; that is, the ag-
gregation of responsible power capable of making
decisions that are something more than a simple
acquiescence to raw pressure or a primitive bartering
of contending claims. At most levels of American
government, the two instruments of responsible representative power for moralizing and homogenizing
group pressures are chief executives, whose legitimacy
normally depends on an external party choice ratified
by a plurality of electoral votes; and legislative leadership, whose legitimacy depends on the sanction of
party caucuses within legislative houses. Anything that

weakens the capacity of those centers of responsible power to accommodate differences, while searching for an overarching public interest testable at elections, undermines the legitimacy and effectiveness of the entire political system.

For a number of reasons, including recent abuses of executive power, administrative violations of due process, the propensity of legislators and officials to overclassify governmental information, and the unreasonable secrecy within which some public business has been conducted, various reform groups have attempted to open the entire system to immediate public scrutiny. By promoting "sunshine laws" ("sunlight purifies as well as illuminates"), reformers have succeeded in many states and at the national level in correcting some of the abuses noted above. In the process, however, the simplistic drafting of rigid sunshine laws has in many places undermined or unduly constrained essential political activity. At some point in the process of public decision making, after various groups have made their demands known, after "participatory democracy" has taken place, temporal and spatial environments must be created that permit responsible authorities to sort out claims and counterclaims, analyze trade-offs, and develop face-saving formulae that optimize a series of inevitably conflicting values. In some circumstances, this cardinal aspect of democratic politics can best take place in the open. But in many cases, enforced openness through indiscriminate sunshine laws simply drives the process underground, or provides interest groups with a monitoring opportunity that they—not the general public or even the press—will exercise, and that inhibits the free give-and-take of honest compromise. Sunshine purifies, but an excess causes cancer.

Inasmuch as the public cannot possibly know everything that is going on, even in the open, the real protection of the public interest rests in holding political authorities responsible for results, not in inhibiting the processes through which decisions are made. If the American public has become so distrustful of its public servants that it has to impose detailed surveillance techniques to monitor every moment of their public behavior, this nation will have designed a system which in truth is the "triumph of technique over purpose." As Edward Levi has put it, "A right of complete confidentiality in government could not only produce a dangerous public ignorance but also destroy the basic representative functions of government. But a duty of complete disclosure would render impossible the effective operations of government."

Similarly, government can be immobilized if demands by any group for participation in the processes of decision making become a euphemism for minority control by veto or disruption. Some weight must always be given to intensity of feeling on the part of special interests (for example, labor; business; agriculture; banking; veterans; education; religious, racial, and ethnic groups), but democracy is meaningless if responsible majorities cannot be formed and given the power to govern. This is why the health of American political parties—the great organizers of pluralities and majorities—is so important. This is why the antiparty sentiments of the American public are so dangerous. America's general ignorance about the significance and the workings of its party system is a defect so serious as to threaten the viability of the entire democratic enterprise.

Majorities, including party majorities, must, of course, rule within the framework of the Constitution. Independent courts, a free press, and ultimately a committed and informed citizenry are the fundamental safeguards of this elaborate and essentially benign system.

These fundamental propositions about power and responsibility must be learned by each new generation. Schools and colleges have a particular responsibility to inform their charges of these basic necessities. But all parts of the polity, including the press, myriad interest groups, political parties, and the government itself, share the burden of instructing citizens in the conditions of preserving freedom in a big democracy. Individual courage and loyalty to high principles must be manifest in abundance in all parts of the complex system if it is to work: individual politicians; individual bureaucrats; individual judges; individual interest-group representatives; individual party workers; individual reporters, commentators, and editors; and individual citizens who are motivated only by a concern for the public weal. But these persons must learn the art of using or influencing the complex and often ponderous machinery of politics and government if they are to make constructive changes in the substance and the procedures of the polity.

The Development of Political Skills

Abstract and general knowledge about the polity is one thing. The skills and attitudes needed to make the polity work are something else. Schools and colleges do not do well at conveying the knowledge. On the matter of skill development, they are woefully deficient. How can the American society educate future generations of leaders (hundreds of thousands of them) and future generations of informed and critical citizens (millions of them) to have the heart, the brains, and the guts to think and to behave responsibly as political beings? The late James Thurber admonished us not to look backward in anger, not forward in fear, but around us in awareness. By and large we have not heeded that advice. We have received little help from our schools and colleges in identifying the skills, mental attitudes, moral philosophies, and social commitments needed for the survival of our democratic values—perhaps even for the survival of the species.

Educational administrators and teachers do not, I think, lack desire to be helpful in the socialization process. Considerable time and attention have been paid by schools to the inculcation of attitudes of patriotism and tolerance and to the underlying political philosophies of our constitutional system. And the best of America's schools, colleges, and universities have stimulated an honest social criticism that has had, I think, an important and healthy influence on both foreign affairs and recent domestic events. But when past and present educational practice is measured against present and future national and international need, an enormous educational gap becomes obvious. Educators have almost totally ignored the development of social and political skills without which even sophisticated attitudes and compendious knowledge are inutile.

What are these social and political skills, and how can they be taught or learned? First, America needs minds that have the skills of relating one thing to another, of seeing connections. Dictionaries contain an uncommon but useful word: "Syndetic," meaning "connecting" or "connective"—the capacity to encompass relationships. Syndetic skills are absolutely essential. There is a compelling need to develop "syndetic" courses and exercises that force students to look for connections—connections between the run-off of farm fertilizers and the death of Lake Erie; connections between the Mideast political crisis and the price of gasoline in Peoria; connections among drought in the Middle West, Soviet economic priorities, and starvation in India; connections between gadgetry and pollution; connections between corruption and inflation; connections between prejudice and domestic crime.

Only if citizens understand the complex ingredients of social causation, and the probabilistic rather than the certain consequences of social choices, will they develop the capacity to solve the problems that beset the nation and the world, or even to live stoically with the maddening trade-offs (e.g., energy vs. environmental priority) that confront decision makers.

Much of America's scholastic and collegiate curriculum needs to be reexamined to see where and how
"syndetic" exercises can be insinuated into existing
materials, how new knowledge can be introduced that
forces students increasingly to reckon with complex
interdependencies. Educators have long sensed this
need, but in view of the probable future, the responses
have been insufficient in both quality and number.

Second, the educational system needs to turn out
generations of negotiators. The past few centuries of
Western history have seen a secular weathering-down
of the great peaks of despotism symbolized by terms
like "divine right" or "absolute monarchy." Orders
do not suffice in a world of manifold epicenters of
power. In a world of 150 separate nations, a myriad
of provincial and local authorities, tens of thousands
of multinational and subnational economic entities,
hundreds of professional and scientific guilds, and
an immense variety of artisan trades, horizontal—not
vertical—communications are the condition of cooperation. Who is willing any longer to be at the beck
and call of either a domineering employer or sovereign
or even a condescending patron? J. H. Elliott reminds
us that this new relationship was symbolized as far
back as the early sixteenth century by the anxious
attempts of that "normally headstrong Pope, Julius
II, to calm down the equally irascible Michelangelo
and induce him to return to Rome to paint the Sistine
ceiling . . . the mere artist and the spiritual ruler of
Christendom now met on equal terms."

And so it is, no matter where we turn. The United
States does not order the Soviet Union around. The
president of General Motors does not order the president of the United Automobile Workers around. Nobody in his right mind orders a plumber around.

If common purposes are to be achieved in a world
of often willful autonomies, legitimate authority must
be coupled with skills of negotiation. These skills
involve rhetorical abilities in the Aristotelian sense—

the ability to persuade (note the comment of Aristotle's great teacher, Plato: "Persuasion, not coercion, is the divine element in the world"). Beyond rhetoric, the negotiating skill also involves both the subtleties and psychic resiliencies associated with the ability to resolve or defuse conflicts—to talk people down from their "highs" of anger and mistrust. Negotiating also involves the most essential of all political talents: the capacity to bargain; to discover areas of agreement; in the nonpejorative sense, to deal.

Except for limited opportunities in student government, we do little in education to prepare young people for the negotiating skills they will need for the appropriate performance of their civic obligations—let alone for the mundane realities of personal and occupational coping. American education needs to create a new facet to the curriculum—a facet that James Coleman would call "action rich"—which exercises regularly the negotiating abilities of young people. Through simulation, role playing, games, in-basket techniques, modified T-groups, and through real participation in the governance of appropriate school and college activities, young people must train their diplomatic muscles. Negotiating skills are the underlying political necessity, not just showing young people how to pull a voting lever.

This necessity for negotiating skills confronts some hardy values that are deeply implanted in the American psyche from childhood on. Americans put a high value on winning, but negotiating implies the value of settling equitably and fairly with *no* winners in the traditional, egocentric sense. Furthermore, negotiating suggests compromise, and we are reared to believe that one should not compromise between right and wrong. The oversimplifications of our bimodal moral perceptions tend to make us reject the very essence of our political process. In a universe of conflict and multiplicity of values, if two people disagree, neither need be wicked. This nation must have an enormous

pool of skilled negotiators if its citizens are to have
world peace and domestic tranquility. Equally important, there must exist a general population prepared
to accept negotiated settlements of tough and emotion-
laden issues.

The Education of Leaders

Fear of the abuses of power has led many people
to the insane conclusion that democracies do not need
leaders equipped with the knowledge and the authority
to govern. The dismal reality is that all too many parts
of this nation's operating polity are in the hands of
amateurs who have neither the knowledge nor the
authority to govern responsibly. "Responsibly" is used
here in both its moral and its political sense. Beyond
educating the general citizenry to understand the
constitutional and political system and to become
familiar with the syndetic and negotiating skills needed to relate to the system and shape it, American
education needs to place very special emphasis on
the preservice and inservice education of its political
leadership.

Unfortunately, there are few useful historical or even
theoretical models on education for political leadership. The cultivation of Plato's "Philosopher Kings,"
the education of Chinese mandarins, the training of
British colonial servants—these come to mind as past
attempts to articulate the special preparation needed
by rulers. But each of these models was essentially
undemocratic. Each had the good of the public at
heart, but that good was to be determined largely by
rulers, not by the ruled.

The agenda of modern public policy is almost
unbelievably complex. Even a generation ago, T.
Swann Harding lamented:

> It is up to congressional committees and then to the
> Congress as a whole to grasp and decide upon the justice
> of appropriations for such projects as: the use of endocrines

to increase egg production; the role of Johne's disease, coccidiosis, and worm parasites in cattle production; the production of riboflavin from milk by-products; spot treatment with soil fumigants for the control of root-knotnematode on melons; the use of mass releases of Macrocentus Ancylivorus to control Oriental fruit moth injury; and the conversion of lactose into methyl acrylate to be polymerized with butadiene for the production of synthetic rubber.

And those matters were cited for their complexity years before space flight, intricate issues of telecommunications, hard trade-offs between economic productivity and environmental protection, subtle links between municipal and international finance, the energy crisis, complex commodity bargains, nuclear threats, and anarchic competition in the partitioning of ocean resources. Disciplinary, multidisciplinary, and professional expertise of the highest order needs to be available to and through our elected and appointed leaders if such issues are to be understood and intelligently resolved. The polity needs the intellectual services and, frequently, the political leadership of lawyers, doctors, biologists, engineers, chemists, foresters, economists, linguists, psychologists, social workers, military and diplomatic specialists, geologists, geographers—the list of needed specializations is as vast as the services and regulatory responsibilities of all of our levels and facets of government. In spite of valiant attempts of some colleges and universities to broaden their law school curricula, to create schools of public administration and public policy, and to launch inservice training courses for government personnel, most disciplinary and professional training in higher education is ill-suited to the cultivation and preparation of democratic leaders. Those who know the rigidities and the vested interests that abound in the academic world will not be surprised by this observation. Yet no issue is of greater consequence to the survival of this nation and of the world than the adequacy of the *generalist* political training of disciplinary and professional specialists in all fields.

Without going into specifics, it may be useful to summarize the insights that have been evolved by those who in the past half century have been charged with developing schools and institutes of public administration and public policy. They have been the persons most directly concerned with education for public leadership. What they have learned may serve those who feel the need to borrow.

Over the past fifty years or so, a number of major trends have been observable. Here, four curricular emphases may be noted: rational management, political process, policy analysis, and clientele service.

The management emphasis, which dominated many of the early programs in public administration—at the Maxwell School at Syracuse and at many land-grant institutions—rested on the assumption that administration and policy were distinct functions of government. A fairly messy, partly ineffable, democratic political process produced goals. The function of "education for the public service" programs was to turn out tidy types who could carry out efficiently and economically the tasks set by untidy but electorally responsible political actors. The courses were labeled budgeting and accounting, personnel administration, planning, organization and methods, the legal framework of administration. More recently, some of this emphasis has reappeared under the guise of Operations Research, Program Planning and Budgeting Systems, and Management by Objectives. The underlying philosophy has not changed: whatever the given task, it can be done more effectively with the help of sophisticated management tools wielded by public-spirited, disinterested generalists.

Of all the public figures in this century, no one did more than Paul Appleby to point out the limitations of the "impartial manager," public service ideal. In his great post-World War II books, *Policy and Administration* and *Morality and Administration,* drawn from his own rich experiences as Undersecretary of Agriculture and as Acting Director of the Bureau of the Budget, Appleby demonstrated that in real life, policy making and public management are inextricably intertwined. Appleby's message was soft but clear: if you want to educate people for the public service, acquaint them with the realities of the political process—with congressional behavior, with human foibles and ambitions, with interest groups, with internecine power struggles, with the court life of the White House, with intergovernmental relations, with negotiations and bargaining and compromise. Public service is not a management science at all, it is a political art—the art of utilizing complex machinery for the accomplishment of political and personal goals.

Programs and schools oriented toward public service careers do not, on the whole, do very well in educating young people in political process sophistication. Impressive books and articles by Paul Appleby, Bertram Gross, David Truman, David Easton, Charles Lindblom, and others, and a number of biographies, novels, case studies, articles, and even plays have provided a good and useful bibliography. But there is something almost temperamental in a generational sense that makes it difficult for many young people to view the accommodations of the political process as moral and as necessary to the survival of a democratic society. (It took me a long time to understand that the reason rain falls on the just and the unjust alike is that he is the same fellow.) It is difficult to conceive of educational programs designed to train for the public service that would not attempt in one way or another to introduce students to the fascinating and perennially unsettling realities of the political process.

The policy analysis emphasis is a fairly recent concept, stemming particularly from Harold Lasswell's seminal work immediately following World War II. Pioneered at the Brookings Institution in the 1920s and at Harvard's Littauer Center in the 1930s with

special attention to macroeconomics, policy studies
now abound in such fields as health, education, energy,
environmental science, foreign affairs, and urbanism.
Policy analysis activities appear more frequently in
the profit and nonprofit think-tanks of the nation than
in universities. Policy science tends to be eclectic in
methodology, although increasing emphasis is placed
on sophisticated quantitative techniques and systems
analysis models. Policy analysis has developed a rich
and partly recondite vocabulary: inputs, outputs, feedback, evaluation, trade-offs, side effects, gaming, re-
gressions, cost/benefit, and so on. It is laden with
seductivity. It is friendly to computer play. It conveys
both the hopes and the dangers of Platonic rationality
in the conduct of the public's business. On occasion
it edges toward demonstrable truths that are politically
compelling. Most of the schools and programs of
public administration and public policy in this nation
spend an increasing amount of time on this only
partially defined field of intellectual emphasis. The
main trouble with much policy analysis work is that
its products are rarely geared to a political world of
unpredictables and crunch. In consequence, political
process insights are especially needed by those who
would pretend to predict, or to influence through
highly rational policy analysis techniques, the vagrant
vectors of public affairs.

All theories of public leadership in a democracy
must be presumed to have the welfare of citizens as
their ultimate goal. Reform movements, like Naderism
and Common Cause, however, and a host of policy-
oriented groups in such fields as health delivery
services, compensatory education, civil rights, environmental protection, and so on, have given new life
to a clientele orientation, both in the sense of participation and of service-effectiveness. This emphasis is
having a perceptible impact upon schools and programs of public affairs, law, business management,
medicine, engineering, and so on. How deep and

fundamental this client orientation really is, I do not pretend to know. Within limits suggested earlier in this chapter, I find it heartening, for it causes students and faculty to focus on public-interest questions too long ignored or taken for granted. It also addresses one of humankind's most difficult and seemingly eternal moral questions: how to organize a polity so that ultimate clients as well as intermediate agents benefit from public wealth—how to ensure that pupils benefit as well as teachers, patients as well as doctors, welfare clients as well as welfare workers.

These then, are four salients for education programs for public service. A judicious mixture of all of them is necessary if, in borrowed and adapted form, they are to assist disciplinary and professional specialists to prepare for the public role that will be thrust upon many of them during their careers: as congressional staff, as lobbyists, as political executives, as judges, as civil servants, as subject-matter specialists for the media. To paraphrase Don K. Price, nothing short of the total resources of the university is adequate to the task of preservice and inservice education for the public service.

The Unfinished Agenda of Governments

Effective public leadership is quite impossible without public confidence in public officials and in the political system. So often citizens view public life through clouded glasses. The public enterprise is far too important to be pulled down by the misdeeds of a few and sensational derogations by the media. Whatever the shortcomings, the public sector has as its ultimate raison d'être such benign goals as:

—to continue and to hasten the process of bringing meaningful work and a fair chance to all our citizens regardless of background;
—to open up and recast our political and economic institutions in order to free people from structural

and procedural bondages that crush creativity and
joy;
—to protect and promote the health of the citizenry;
—to revamp, in the spirit of my late colleague and
friend, Richard T. Frost, the penal system of this
country in order to destroy the last vestiges of
medieval torture from our midst;
—to stimulate the future evolution and reworking
of our educational and cultural services so that
they are available to all ages and types of people,
and so that we can once again learn to revere
the creative work of inspired and gifted human
beings;
—to remind us that the squalor and famine and
crowdedness of three-quarters of the world is an
intolerable burden, not only on the victims, but
on the immediate conscience and long-range safety of the prosperous;
—to work unceasingly for the eradication of war
as a means of settling international as well as
domestic disputes, and to discover those mecha-
nisms of peaceful conflict resolution that can give
surcease to the nuclear anxieties of the human
race;
—to clean up our oceans and streams and soiled
winds and tawdry cities;
—to discover energy sources that will enhance rather
than pollute the biosphere;
—to set aside and regulate areas of special beauty
and felicity for the long-run enjoyment of the
whole human race.

Some of these desirable goals can be pursued by
interested citizens within their local communities
through volunteer action; through serving on boards,
commissions, and study groups; through partisan political activity; through achieving elected office. This
is the level of active citizen participation that comes
closest to the ancient ideal of direct democracy. For
most people, the local community or neighborhood

is the first effective laboratory for political involvement, for political education by doing. Schools and
colleges have a responsibility to communicate and to
underscore to young and old the importance of local
political involvement. It can be satisfying to the
individual. It can help to solve local problems. It is
the "boot camp" for larger political engagements.

Most of the great issues that affect our lives, however,
are state, national, or global in character. Here the
enhanced education of political leaders and policy
specialists is of the greatest moment. Here, the essential
functions of the larger public are to keep informed,
to hold leaders accountable, to develop a capacity for
steadfastness through trials, and to elevate the sense
of community and civility that Walter Lippmann once
called the public philosophy.

The transiency of individual lives can be interpreted
as nature's assurance of newness and aliveness and
fleeting wonder in the world. But there is an ancient
wisdom that survives all the passings of human
beings—great and small. It is the wisdom that forms
our sense of worth at its highest; it is the wisdom
of Emerson's "incessant affirmatives"; the wisdom
of those poets and prophets who have in fact caught
the patriot dream that sees beyond the years our
"alabaster cities gleam undimmed by human tears"—
who have always known that this is one world and
that we are in truth one people, and who have always
sensed that beneath the superficial skulduggeries and
pettinesses of the human race is an unquenchable
hunger for beauty and goodness and truth.

Releasing this still unrealized promise of the human
race is the ultimate reason for, and condition of, a
civilized polity. Ultimately only administratively effective and politically responsible government can
secure freedom: and only freedom can permit the
human spirit to evolve to its next higher destiny.

> For what avail, the plow or sail,
> Or land, or life, if freedom fail?

7

Implications and Directions

The preceding chapters have identified some basic realities in late twentieth-century America—bedrock existential realities that call for a restatement or a reformulation of the nation's educational purposes. Scattered throughout are references to formal educational institutions and programs and to informal educative agents and facilities that can contribute to those educational purposes. No attempt has been made to articulate a strategy of educational change or to construct rigid assignments directed to various segments of the educational system, nor will such an attempt be made.

My hope has been that readers who agree with one or more of the formulations herein will take stock of the proximate institutions or programs with which they are affiliated to ask seriously, What can we do from where we are with the levers we can use to make a difference? The American educational system has always had the virtue of latent pluralism, even though its predominant structures and curricular paradigms have been quite standardized in practice. The opportunity for local initiatives and creative salients still remains, especially now that the educational functions of nontraditional educative agents and agencies are being increasingly recognized and accepted. In sum, it is hoped that this study will stimulate—just as it reflects—widespread and diverse responses to the problems and opportunities identified.

There are, however, a few comments I must make

about implications and directions that seem to emerge logically from the preceding pages. They are offered tentatively. Their purpose is to stimulate, not to direct, the reader's own reactions and responses.

Learning and Education

A commonly employed definition of an educated person is one who has learned to learn. It can be argued that if our formal educational system were doing its job effectively, people exposed to its instruction would need no other educational services. Tapping the rich resources of knowledge and skill-development that abound in our society, those formally educated in our schools and colleges would all be self-starters and masters of their own fate. Turning to books, the *Reader's Guide to Periodical Literature, Psychological Abstracts,* a talented neighbor, a sympathetic foreman, an experienced executive, the *Encyclopedia Britannica,* the U.S. Government Printing Office, and *Popular Mechanics,* lifelong learners would need only time and initiative to cope with any and all problems that might come their way.

It seems clear, of course, that with or without our formal educational system, people would in fact learn. They always have. Experience is each individual's most effective tutor. In this sense, all of us are life's apprentices. We learn from hot stoves and cold rejections, from parents and siblings, from friends and enemies, from co-workers and supervisors, from TV and radio, from newspapers and gossip, from indigestion and aching backs.

But judging by the quality of our lives and the critical strains that have started to rip the fabric of our civilization, we are still dangerously ignorant. Hit-and-miss learning is obviously inadequate. That is why the central focus of this monograph is the educative instruments—human and inanimate, formal and informal, actual and potential—that need to be consciously fashioned or refashioned if lifelong learning is to be effectively and continuously catalyzed for most people. A series of perverse problems of motivation, lack of confidence, preoccupation, conflicting advice, and ignorance inhibit the self-learning capacity in all of us. If this were not so, once initially schooled, we should all be as happy as kings were once supposed to be; we should all be able to construct a good society in perpetuity.

The resources for self-learning in our society are prodigious. We do not use them well because we have not worked hard enough to improve the educational institutions, and to develop the educational services, that are the keys to the kingdom of individual growth over a long life, and to the maintenance and advancement of a civilized polity.

Retooling the Schools

During the middle decades of the twentieth century, expanding enrollments, economic prosperity, space competition with the Soviets, parental enthusiasms, and political leadership greatly expanded the number and range of school facilities and programs. Wealthy school districts built comprehensive plants, many of them replete with elaborate science and home economics laboratories, art and music studios, swimming pools, gymnasiums and playing fields, professional stage equipment, TV and radio centers, and vocational, technical, and paraprofessional shops and training simulators. In retrospect, such schools appeared to assume responsibility for all aspects of human development. Under one model of America's educational future, presumably the millenium would be reached if all schools or school systems could command resources adequate to the universalization of these educational palaces.

Unfortunately, few of America's young people have had the advantages of enriched, campus-style comprehensive schools. As Ralph Tyler and others point out, 20 percent of this nation's school population do not learn to read, write, or handle mathematics. The children of the poor—many of them housed in vandalized, dilapidated structures located in crime-ridden, central-city ghettos—are educationally victimized by a background of family impoverishment and a foreground of noise, fear, and disruption. They lack the learning environments needed for them to master basic cognitive skills; they often lack the adult and peer role models and the economic expectations needed to motivate them out of their hopelessness. Schools are mirrors of their surrounding communities. In a modern version of Gresham's law, custody has driven out learning.

Between these extremes, thousands of schools do the best they can for middle-class youngsters but operate with limited facilities in the face of shrinking enrollments and shrinking budgets. In common with schools of the rich and of the poor, they tend to reflect confusion about purposes and priorities. And any notion that their staffs and resources be suddenly expanded to accommodate all the basic and instrumental purposes of education suggested herein could meet only bemused laughter, cynicism, or wistfulness.

Even the few educational palaces of the 1950s and 1960s were locked into curricular traditions and teacher preparations that precluded their addressing many of the purposes of education that now seem so important. Then, as always, people learned through a wide variety of experiences and contacts: family life, peer interaction, the media, on-the-job training, military service, camps, street playgrounds, religious and social service institutions, and so on. As Ralph Tyler has put it, "Teachers for the schools were employed not to teach everything young people needed to learn but to concentrate their efforts on the fruits of scholarship, reading, writing, mathematics, history, and other subjects that appeared to offer knowledge, skills, and points of view that could serve as important resources for the individual."

With all this as background, it is difficult to see how the education of the young can be significantly improved in the absence, first, of reeducation of professional teachers and educational administrators, and second, of imaginative articulations of inschool activities to educative resources in the larger community.

In relation to the children of the urban poor, an additional comment is needed. Most of the major central cities of America are becoming minority ghettos. In spite of court decisions over a quarter of a century, this nation's metropolitan areas are largely patchwork quilts of separate and unequal educational opportunity. There are more preponderantly segregated schools in this nation in the 1970s than there were in the 1950s. While judicial and legislative instruments attempt to find a long-term redress for the patent grievances of urban minorities, short-term educational solutions call for heroic acts of invention and financial underwriting addressed to the locked-in educational environments of the poor. At the very least, attempts should be made to decentralize learning facilities with a variety of safe miniquarters. Superbly prepared teachers and teacher aides should be provided in sufficient numbers to help the children of the poor overcome their familial and economic handicaps.

On the larger canvas, how can school teachers and supervisors be reeducated at the same time that school activities are linked to the educative resources of the larger community? And how can these changes take place without breaking the bank of educational finance? Experiments are going on all over the nation. Drawing from these experiments, let me propose a possible model, not for universal adoption, but as a way of inducing other models from disparate readers.

Suppose the school week were reduced from five days to four. In many school districts, this shift would automatically save transportation costs one day a week. Suppose the money saved were put into teacher-run teachers centers devoted to creative inservice education activities, where existing curricular content and pedagogic techniques could be reviewed and improved by the teachers themselves. The centers could be based in the schools, or in nearby universities, or in independent settings. Every Friday, teachers would learn instead of teach. In part, they would learn from each other. In part, they would use their teachers centers as meeting grounds for conversations with selected parents, supervisors, administrators, school board members, professional specialists, and leaders in various occupations with whom they share an educational responsibility. With the cooperation of those other members of the larger community, teachers would consider purposes of education that seem important to the larger community. They would work on the development of techniques and materials that would help to modify existing practices and course content. They would help to define which aspects of education could best be handled within the school and which aspects should involve other educative instruments in the larger society.

In the meantime, what would pupils and students be doing on the fifth day—out of school? They would be doing all kinds of things. Slow learners might spend the day being tutored in basic skills by slightly older peers, who in turn might receive compensation in the form of scholarship credits held in escrow until their college years. Volunteer parents and grandparents might play and fantasize with primary-age pupils and take young people on nature walks or on trips to museums, airports, factories, TV studios. High school students might have apprenticeship experiences in a labor union or work experience in an industry or in

neglected social, recreational, and health services of
the community—these opportunities orchestrated by
Community-Education-Work Councils of the kind
recommended by Willard Wirtz. Some of these assignments might involve cash payments in the form of
part-time wages or salaries; other assignments might
be recompensed by postsecondary scholarships or
fellowship grants.

For the gifted, breaking the five-day academic lockstep could be a highly liberating and supportive
experience—opening up possibilities for independent
study and for creative endeavors not readily available
in most formal academic and scholastic settings.

Performing arts centers might well reserve their
facilities on Friday for budding musicians, dancers,
and actors.

The details here are not important. The general
direction is. Teachers must be given the chance to
recharge their batteries and improve their knowledge
and skills; community leaders of all kinds must be
encouraged to participate in the process of redefining
educational purposes; young people must be exposed
to the educative resources and to friendly peer and
adult models in the larger community. Since much
of the involvement of the larger community would
involve the volunteer services of adults, and since
the suggested services and employments of youth
would be no greater burden on public treasuries than
alternatives of welfare, unemployment compensation,
or prison, additional costs of such a program to the
taxpayers would be minimal. And the results could
be heartening indeed: the quality of life could be
enhanced for teachers; pupils could find heightened
psychic satisfaction in "action-rich" additions to their
educational experiences; a vast number of older students and adults could serve as instructors and role
models to young people starved for healthy inspira-
tions. New life and new public support could be given

to numbers of persons (including unemployed teachers) and to cultural and civic enterprises presently underutilized and underfinanced.

Recent experience with a four-day week indicates no penalty whatsoever in lowered student achievement in basic skills.

The Role of Colleges and Universities

There are more than 3,000 colleges and universities in the United States. They vary greatly in size, governance, and program. Graduate universities—public and private—have had, and continue to have, standard-setting functions for quality work in advanced research and in preparing exceptionally well qualified young people for the learned professions. Four-year undergraduate colleges have provided, and will continue to provide, a rich smörgasbord of postsecondary intellectual opportunities—both career specific and broadly cultural. Most two-year colleges have emphasized, and will continue to emphasize, vocational and technical as well as liberal arts and paraprofessional training. An increasing number of institutions of postsecondary education of all kinds and sizes are reaching out to the adult community—offering both credit and noncredit courses in a dazzling variety of cultural and technical fields.

If the basic insights in this monograph have any validity, however, few colleges and universities have addressed themselves to the range of individual and societal needs that mark the existential realities of the last decades of the twentieth century: the need for long-life education tied to the predictabilities of stages of human development; the need for increased attention to "mastery skills" to overcome the draining anxieties of existential coping; the need to prepare people for the repetitiveness and routineness of most work, and the importance of creating new forms, modes, and definitions of work; the need to educate people in the negotiating arts, syndetic skills, and moral philosophies of effective political participation in a technologically advanced and structurally ponderous democratic system; and, above all, the need to help people to have truly creative engagements with the taunting and frequently fretful world of the free self. This last needs a special underscoring. If, as recent data and analysis have demonstrated, the income gap between college-degree holders and those without degrees is narrowing, higher education can no longer justify its activities alone on economic grounds. For the overwhelming majority of its students, higher education can only hold out the possibility that collegiate and university study will improve the quality of existence for the individual and ultimately for society as a whole. But that promise is hollow unless higher education takes its rhetoric seriously and works aggressively at those curricular and pedagogic reforms that can in fact improve the quality of human life. Surely the place to start is in reworking and restructuring the tired, often archaic components of the "liberal arts" curriculum. Liberal learning must become, in fact and theory, learning that both liberates the free self and increases the individual's sense of civic duty. I have tried in Chapters V and VI to suggest desirable directions for those needed changes.

All those associated with higher education must keep in mind that college and university trained people in *all* disciplinary and professional fields constitute the society's basic cadre of teachers. Lionel Trilling contended that the most loving of human relationships is the pedagogic relationship. Higher education's most significant service may well be that of inculcating in the minds of future doctors, engineers, lawyers, scientists, clergy, social workers, business executives, economists, politicians, journalists, and reformers that they, not just graduates of schools of education, have the obligation and opportunity to be lifelong teachers. For if education is a ubiquitous need, all of us must participate in the processes of learning and teaching.

Those with advanced training and education have a special pedagogic responsibility. In general, most of the improvements in the nonformal educative instruments in the American society (TV, radio, museums, libraries, union apprenticeship programs, professions, industry, government, publishing houses) will depend heavily on the creative contributions of those who have had the advantage of a college or university education.

The Need for Educational Brokers

If America is to move toward an educative society in which all of its myriad educative institutions and instruments, formal and informal, play a dynamic and constructive role, one very special gap must be filled. The society will need a new breed of communicators and catalysts: educational counselors and facilitators who can become informed brokers between educational demand and educational supply. In part, the purposes of education have not been approximated in this society because there has been a breakdown in market communications. The diversity of educational offerings and opportunities in this nation is truly astounding. High school dropouts can get diplomas through GED examinations, correspondence courses, and "external diploma" programs; college credits can be achieved in part through external examinations and the assessment of experience; TV and radio courses are parts of many university extension programs; the military, labor unions, and industry are deeply involved in preservice and inservice training; in large metropolitan areas, museums, libraries, churches, performing arts centers, community centers, provide a variety of cultural facilities, programs, and materials. Proprietary schools provide training in a variety of occupational skills. College and university extension divisions offer a range of credit and noncredit courses on and off campus in almost every conceiv-

able subject for almost every conceivable segment of
the society.

Part of the task of approximating the purposes of
education as formulated here is to reform curricular
content and pedagogic techniques. But part of the
task is to link those persons who have educational
needs to the extraordinary range of educational opportunities that already exist in this society. Appropriate
educational and occupational counseling services are
needed at all levels, but particularly for adults.

There are no instant recipes for improving the human
lot, no patent medicines, no easy fixes. It is unreasonable to expect a sudden and universal "greening of
America." For some, the struggle for meaning, for
happiness, may not be worth the effort. But for an
increasing number of Americans, a new perspective
is possible on the chances of enhancing the quality
of personal existence and achieving a greater measure
of social justice at home and abroad. The educational
path suggested in this volume is arduous. It involves
self-discipline and steadfastness. It cannot be traveled
successfully without company, or without leaders who
believe in themselves and in their fellows. But for
those who set about searching for ways, through
education, to enhance the quality of human stages
of development, enrich the various aspects of the
existential wheel, and improve the functioning and
the equity of the enveloping polity, the dividends may
be rich indeed—in results achieved and as a function
of the unending search itself.

If the essential political need in America in the early
years of its third century is for a new sense of
community, perhaps the informed networks of a truly
educative society can begin the process of linking
people together—old and young, rich and poor, white
and colored ethnics, humanists and scientists, artists
and technicians. One thing seems clear. If it is true
that enhancing the quality of the stages of develop-

ment, the existential wheel, and the enveloping polity is to constitute the high purposes of the American educational system in the years ahead, Americans surely need each other.

Bibliographical Notes

This monograph springs in large part from personal observation, experience, and reflection. Much of it is based on insights derived from active participation in both education and politics over several decades. In addition, as the youngest of eight children, I have had the advantage of watching older brothers and sisters and their offspring cope with the stages of development and problems of living—and have learned much from their example. My own experience as a spouse and a parent has been educative, especially because of the understanding and good humor of my wife and children. To my parents, now dead a quarter of a century, I owe special gratitude: to my mother, for her love of words; to my father, for his love of beauty in all its manifestations.

My years as a university teacher and educational administrator have been mostly joyous and always informative. Of my nonuniversity roles, I have derived insights about both education and politics from my experiences as mayor of a city; as an administrative assistant to a United States Senator; as a member of New York State's Board of Regents; and, since 1973, as vice president of the American Council on Education in Washington.

I have read as I have taught—and as I have run. My wife and my daughter Lois spent a number of weeks in 1975 culling and summarizing a literature unfamiliar to me but patently important to the development of this monograph. Rather than clutter each page and each chapter with a myriad footnotes, I have attempted in these bibliographical notes to select a few major sources that have been particularly informative and helpful.

Preface

There are a number of excellent surveys of the history of educational and political theory. For this essay, I have drawn special nourishment from the overviews of George H. Sabine's classic text, *A History of Political Theory* (Harrap, 1937), and S. J. Curtis and M. A. Boultwood, *A Short History of Educational Ideas* (University Tutorial Press, 2nd Edition, 1956). Although I found both John Dewey and A. N. Whitehead less helpful as articulators of educational purposes than I had hoped, Dewey's use of the term "growth" and Whitehead's concern with the "usefulness" of education helped to stimulate my thinking. See Joseph Ratner (ed.), *Intelligence in the Modern World: John Dewey's Philosophy* (The Modern Library, 1939), especially pp. 627–630, 673, and 675; and A. N. Whitehead, *The Aims of Education* (Macmillan, 1929), *passim;* note, for example, in Whitehead, p. 2, "Pedants sneer at an education which is useful. But if education is not useful, what is it?" For my purposes, by far the most valuable summation of educational goal-setting in the United States in the past century is Lawrence A. Cremin, *The Transformation of the School* (Vintage, 1964). See also an incisive summary of educational purposes by R. Freeman Butts prepared as a contribution to the 1975 National Forum of the College Entrance Examination Board.

The slipperiness of the term "the public interest" was first remarked in this century by Walter Lippmann in his great work, *Public Opinion* (Macmillan, 1922).

My general description of the condition of America as it enters its third century is based upon direct observation, conversations, survey-research data, periodic literature, and a few key books. Especially provocative have been the fall, 1975 issue of the *Public Interest* devoted to *The American Commonwealth;* Richard N. Goodwin, *The American Condition* (Doubleday, 1974); Carl Solberg, *Riding High: America in the Cold War* (Mason Charter, 1974); Peter L. Berger et. al, *The Homeless Mind* (Random, 1973); E. J. Kahn, Jr., *The American People: The Findings of the 1970 Census* (Weybright and Talley, 1974); and Robert A. Nisbet, *Community and Power* (Oxford University Press, 1967) and *Twilight of Authority* (Oxford University Press, 1975).

The parlous state of the world has been described in Cassandra-like terms by Robert L. Heilbroner in *An Inquiry into the Human Prospect* (Norton, 1974) and Donella H. Meadows, et. al, in *Limits to Growth: A Report for the Club of Rome's Project on the Predicament of Mankind* (Universe, 1974). For a more optimistic view, see the articles and pamphlets of Harlan Cleveland emanating from the Aspen Institute in the spring and summer of 1975, especially *Planetary Bargains.*

The Bedrock Realities

My appreciation goes to Lawrence A. Cremin for suggesting the key term "creative engagements" in the first of my three key purposes, and to Israel Scheffler, Samuel Halperin, and James Browne for underscoring the social and political responsibilities of education reflected in my third purpose.

Most of the questions raised under the rubric of "some of history's toughest philosophical issues" are hardy perennials in moral philosophy. William Butler Yeats in his poem, *The Choice,* raises one of the most difficult problems of existence: does the concentration and single-minded devotion needed to produce excellence in any field mean that a person must abjure the altruism and the manifestations of caring usually associated with "perfection of life."

The late E. E. Schattschneider was, for many years,

chairman of the Department of Government at Wesleyan. He was also president of the American Political Science Association. A gifted teacher, his parables and aphorisms informed and inspired all who knew him. The education of Plato's "Guardians" is to be found in Book II of the *Republic*. I have used the translation by B. Jowett (Oxford, 1924). The quotation from Pliny the Younger is to be found in Curtis and Boulton, *op. cit.*, p. 47.

The first volume of Cremin's trilogy is titled, *American Education: The Colonial Experience 1607-1783* (Harper and Row, 1970).

Education and the Stages of Development

Although many writers have increased my understanding of human stages of development, I am particularly indebted to Cyril O. Houle for his wise counsel and his sage writings on the subject. One of the best summations of the development of life-cycle theory is to be found in his article, "The Changing Goals of Education in the Perspective of Lifelong Learning," *International Review of Education,* Unesco Institution for Education, 1974, pp. 430-445.

I found the reference to Kierkegaard in Robert Coles, *Erik H. Erikson: The Growth of His Work* (Little, Brown, 1970), p. 138. Coles' first chapter is a moving tribute to the place of Kierkegaard in the development of modern psychoanalysis.

Carl G. Jung's essay is to be found in *Collected Works,* Vol. 8, "Structure and Dynamics of the Psyche" (Princeton University Press, 1969), pp. 387-403. Charlotte Bühler's, *Der Menschliche Les benslauf als psychologishes Problem* (S. Hirzel, 1933) is mentioned by most bibliographers in this field. I have found her chapter "The Human Life Cycle" in *Psychology for Contemporary Living* (Hawthorn Books, 1968), pp. 127-265, particularly helpful. See also her book *The Course of Human Life: A Study of Goals in the Humanistic Perspective* (Springer, 1968). Erikson's most succinct exposition of his views on the life cycle is to be found in *Childhood and Society* (Norton, 1964). See also *Identity and the Life Cycle: Selected Papers* (International University Press, 1967), Vol. I. Most of his writings are, of course, germane. His psychobiographies of Luther and Gandhi, for example, are studded with insights into their personality changes over time. See Coles, *op. cit.* for an excellent summary of Erikson's work. My personal contacts with Erikson have been few but extremely rewarding. The theme of my Sir John Adams lecture at the University of California, Los Angeles in 1971 on "Education and the Pursuit of Happiness" was a direct result of his personal encouragement. Conversations with him at meetings of the National Academy of Education, as well as my reading of his works, helped to focus my attention on the importance of the stages of development as an existential base for a restatement of educational purposes.

Among the Americans who have made special contributions to this growing field of interest, articles and books by the following have been particularly useful to me: Robert J. Havighurst, "History of Developmental Psychology: Socialization and Personality Development Through the Life Span," in *Life-Span Developmental Psychology: Personality and Socialization,* edited by Paul B. Baltes and K. Warner Schaie (Academic Press, 1973); Bernice L. Neugarten, especially (ed.) *Middle Age and Aging: A Reader in Social Psychology* (University of Chicago Press, 1968); Roger Gould, especially "Adult Life Stages: Growth Toward Self-Tolerance," *Psychology Today*, February, 1975, pp. 74–78; Cyril O. Houle, *op cit.* Others who have worked or are working on this frontier include Theodore Lidz, Daniel Levinson, and George Vaillant.

In the original outline of this monograph, Piaget was given a far larger place. The reason for reducing the references to him has nothing to do with the importance of his work, but to a growing realization on my part, stimulated by critical judgments by H. Thomas James and David Clark, that Piaget's cognitive "buddings" were of a different order of conceptualization from life-cycle theories. For an excellent critique of Piaget's work see Herbert Ginsburg and Silvia Opper, *Piaget's Theory of Intellectual Development: An Introduction* (Prentice-Hall, 1969), and J. McV. Hunt, "The Impact and Limitations of the Giant of Developmental Psychology," in David Elkind and John H. Flavell, *Studies in Cognitive Development: Essays in Honor of Jean Piaget* (Oxford University Press, 1969), pp. 3–56.

A reference to the Doubting Thomas's of life-cycle theory is to be found in Cyril O. Houle, *op cit.,* pp. 431–2.

The list of "widely agreed upon" statements about the importance of early nurture is my own montage drawn from a number of sources. In addition to sources already mentioned, the writings of Benjamin Bloom, Bruno Bettelheim, Jerome Bruner, and Uri Bronfenbrenner seem to me especially impressive.

The statistics for day-care centers are firmer than those for nursery schools. The former come from the National Center of Educational Statistics, Department of Health, Education, and Welfare. There are no firm figures for the latter. NCES has a 1974 figure of 1,603,000 for enrollment in nursery schools for ages 3, 4, and 5. I have arbitrarily divided that figure by 30 as a reasonable average for enrollments for nursery school.

The importance of the family in child rearing is beautifully summarized in "The Family: First Instructor and Persuasive Guide," *Teachers College Record,* December, 1974. Note particularly the essays by Leichter, Getzels, Cremin, and Bronfenbrenner. In the early 1970s, the schools of Brookline, Massachusetts, undertook an experiment called Brookline Early Education Project based upon the assumption that "a child's future intelligence, social competence, and general ability to learn are all largely determined before the age of 3." See Maya Pines, "Parent and Child: Head Head Start," *New York Times Magazine,* October 26, 1975, and an unpublished project description available through Dr. Donald E. Pierson, director.

I am indebted to Bruno Bettelheim, in a presentation he made to the National Academy of Education in 1965, for insights into the socializing impact of the kibbutz.

There is a vast literature on the problems of adolescence. Erikson, *Identity: Youth and Crisis* (Norton, 1968), is an important basic work. See also his "Reflections on the Dissent of Contemporary Youth," *Daedalus,* Vol. 99, No. 1, 1970, pp. 154-176. Kenneth Keniston's insightful essay, "Youth: A New Stage of Life," *American Scholar,* Vol. 39, autumn, 1970, pp. 631-54, has received deserved attention. For my purposes, the most useful general work was James S. Coleman (chairman), *Youth: Transition to Adulthood—Report on Youth of the President's Science Advisory Committee* (University of Chicago Press, 1974). This contains an excellent bibliography. For a more recent and quite disturbing analysis of late adolescence see Herbert Hendin, "The New Anomie," *Change,* November, 1975, pp. 24-29.

Erikson's description of the problems of middle age are to be found in *Childhood and Society, op. cit.* Bühler's reference to the middle-age "climacterum" is found in her *Psychology for Contemporary Living, op. cit.* There is a growing literature on middle age. I have relied very heavily upon the writings of Bernice L. Neugarten, especially including the key collection of essays edited by her, *Middle Age and Aging: A Reader in Social Psychology* (University of Chicago, 1968). See particularly her essay in this volume entitled "Adult Personality"; see also the contributions of Howard S. Becker and Raymond G. Kuhler. Gail Sheehy has written a sensitive article on middle age, "Catch-30 and Other Predictable Crises of Growing

Up Adult," *New York Magazine,* February 18, 1974, pp. 30-44.

Again, the writings on old age are increasingly voluminous. Neugarten's *Middle Age and Aging, op. cit.,* has a number of valuable essays. See particularly those of Murray and Epstein; Rose; and Reichard, Linser, and Petersen. Wayne Dennis' article, "Creative Productivity Between the Ages of 20 and 80 Years," is an excellent survey of those creative capacities that appear to be vital well into old age. For a more extended discussion of this issue and of cognitive capacities that endure throughout adult life, see *Never Too Old to Learn,* Academy for Educational Development, June, 1974; and Paul B. Baltes and K. Warner Schaie, "The Myth of the Twilight Years," *Psychology Today,* March, 1974, pp. 35-40.

The relationship of middle age behaviors to old age realities is reported in a prodigious linear study by Henry S. Maas and Joseph A. Kuypers, *From Thirty to Seventy: A Forty-Year Longitudinal Study of Adult Life-Styles and Personality* (Jossey-Bass, 1974).

On what might happen to the length of old age if cancer, heart disease, and stroke are eliminated, see Leonard Hayflick, "Why Grow Old," the *Stanford Magazine,* spring-summer, 1975, pp. 36-43.

For insights into the back-to-school movement among the old, see Catherine C. Davis, "Fairhaven's Senior Freshmen," *American Education,* May, 1975, pp. 3-10; and *Saturday Review,* "Lifelong Learning," September 20, 1975, *passim.*

Coping

Appropriate annotations for this chapter are particularly difficult. The basic sources are the introspections and observations of living, and decades of reading— including the occasional perusing of family and women's journals in dentists' and doctors' offices and on airplanes. A few references are, however, in order. An interesting survey of how both upper- and lower-income groups allocate their time during the working hours of the week is to be found in Richard K. Brail and F. Stuart Chapin, Jr., "Activity Patterns of Urban Residents," *Environment and Behavior,* Vol. 5, 1973, pp. 163-187.

The first report on life adjustment stemmed from a 1947 National Conference of the Commission on Life Adjustments for Youth. See *Vitalizing Secondary Education: Education for Life Adjustment,* Bulletin No. 3 (U.S. Government Printing Office, 1951). A second report from the Commission appeared in 1954. The sections of these reports dealing with work, family relationships, and consumerism are worth renewed attention.

Cyril O. Houle's comment on health and illness was made in a marginal note commenting on an early version of the manuscript to this book. For further information on the Breslow study regarding the relationship between good health habits and increased longevity see N. Beloc, "Relationship of Health Practices and Mortality," *Preventive Medicine,* 1973, Vol. 2, pp. 67-81.

The ability of adult Americans to cope with personal and family logistics was studied by a University of Texas team in the mid-1970s. A summary report, *Adult Functional Competency,* was issued in March, 1975. It claims that twenty percent of American adults are essentially unable to cope. Only half of the American adults can be considered truly competent in a functional sense. For further information, write to Adult Performance Level Project, Dr. Norvell Northcutt, Project Director, University of Texas at Austin. These findings are reinforced in a study by the National Assessment of Educational Progress which found that less than half of young adults could determine the most economical size of a product, only ten percent of teen-agers and twenty percent of young adults could correctly calculate a taxi fare, and only one percent of 17-year-olds and sixteen percent of adults could balance a checkbook. Fur further details write to the Education Commission of the States, Denver, Colorado.

On consumer education, the federal government is beginning to stir. See Public Law 93-380, the "Education Amendments of 1974," which provides for a Consumer Education Program. The U.S. Office of Education is authorized to fund projects "designed to help individuals make informal, rational decisions about consumer transactions." See *HEW News*, November 26, 1975. Law in a Free Society is a project of the State Bar of California in cooperation with the Schools of Law of the University of California and University Extension, University of California, Los Angeles. It is perhaps the most sophisticated of literally hundreds of curriculum development projects in America designed to increase school children's understanding of the legal framework of American life.

On the psychological tensions of daily life, I have derived special insights through reading the works of R. D. Laing, especially *Politics of Experience* (Pantheon, 1967), and *Knots* (Pantheon, 1971).

A useful work on the issue of generalized problem solving is George V. Coehlo, David A. Hamberg, and John E. Adams (eds.), *Coping and Adaptation* (Basic Books, 1974); note particularly Chapter 13, "Coping and Adaptation: Steps Toward a Synthesis of Biological and Social Prospectives." The University of California, Los Angeles has developed a Creative Problem Solving Program that has attracted wide attention. For further information write to Architecture Building 1118, UCLA, Los Angeles, California 90024. Although directed largely at solving societal problems, many of the skills featured in the program have equal meaning for personal and family coping.

The quotation from Elma Lewis is from "Words I Live By," *Pictorial Living Coloroto Magazine*, July 27, 1975, p. 5.

David Riesman's interest in "mastery" was conveyed

to me in a panel discussion on my chapter outline at Harvard on June 9, 1975.

Work

A number of writings have been particularly useful to me in the development of this chapter. Chapters three and four of Hannah Arendt's *The Human Condition* (University of Chicago Press, 1958) are excellent statements of the distinction between "labor" and "work." Thomas F. Green's *Work, Leisure, and the American Schools* (Random, 1968) raises even richer distinctions. A. Dale Tussing, "The Future of Jobs, Work, and Leisure," Educational Policy Research Center, Syracuse University Research Corporation (mimeo), August, 1973, is a stunning essay on the changing mix of work and leisure in the American society. Peter L. Berger (ed.), *The Human Shape of Work* (Regnery, 1973), compares a variety of jobs in terms of their rewards and strains. James O'Toole (ed.), *Work and the Quality of Life: Resource Papers for Work in America* (MIT, 1974), contains excellent essays on various aspects of the matters treated superficially in this chapter. Willard Wirtz, *The Boundless Resource: A Prospectus for an Education-Work Policy* (New Republic, 1975), is a graceful and practical statement of possible policy options for creating jobs and for relating education to employment through community councils. Robert J. Havighurst has a perceptive essay on the relationship between changing societal patterns and the world of work. See his "Social Roles, Work, Leisure, and Education," in Carl Eisdorfer and McPowell Lawton (eds.), *The Psychology of Adult Development and Aging* (American Psychological Association, 1973).

The call for "career education" is particularly associated with Sidney P. Marland, Jr. when he was U.S. Commissioner of Education in the early 1970s. See Marland (ed.), *Essays on Career Education* (Northwest Regional Educational Laboratory, 1973) and Marland,

Career Education: A Proposal for Reform (McGraw, 1975). See also Kenneth Hoyt, *Career Education: Contributions to an Evolving Concept* (Olympus, 1975), Joel H. Magisos (ed.), *Career Education,* the third yearbook of the American Vocational Association, 1973.

For a popularized version of the declining economic value of higher education, see Caroline Bird, *The Case Against College* (McKay, 1975). For a more systematic and scholarly approach see the article by Richard Freeman and Herbert Hollomon on "The Declining Value of College Going," *Change,* September, 1975, pp. 24–31.

The source for references to youth unemployment in the mid-1970s is Wirtz, *op. cit.,* Chapter I.

For interesting insights into the world of underemployment, see two articles by James O'Toole, "The Reserve Army of the Underemployed," *Change,* May, 1975 and June, 1975.

I am grateful for the help of the Roper Center in Williamstown, Massachusetts, in providing access to relevant Gallup Polls from 1963 to 1973 that surveyed job satisfaction. I have also used the Gallup Opinion Index Report No. 94, *Job Satisfaction and Productivity,* April, 1973. A recent examination of assembly line trauma can be found in Barbara Garson, *All the Livelong Day: The Meaning and Demeaning of Routine Work* (Doubleday, 1975). See also, Daniel Yankelovich, "Turbulence in the Working World: Angry Workers, Happy Grads," *Psychology Today,* December, 1974; and Edmund Faltermayer, "Who Will Do the Dirty Work?" *Fortune,* January, 1974, pp. 132–138.

The Berger quotation comes from his book *The Human Shape of Work, op. cit.,* p. 221.

The most significant legislative initiative in the area of full employment policy in recent years has been the so-called Hawkins-Humphrey Full Employment Bill, HR50 (Subcommittee on Equal Opportunities print of March 20, 1975).

For an important statement on how full employment might help limit rather than exacerbate inflation, see Peter Barnes, *Working Papers,* Fall, 1975.

See also, *Full Employment as a National Goal,* Proceedings of the 64th National Urban League Conference, 1975.

Perhaps the most impressive single force in keeping alive the issue of the importance of basic skills is the Council for Basic Education in Washington, D.C. Its hand-sized pamphlets have a readership of influentials across the nation.

The updating of people in their jobs—especially members of the learned professions—is a special interest of Cyril O. Houle. See, for example, "The Lengthened Line," *Perspectives in Biology and Medicine* (University of Chicago, Autumn, 1967); "To Learn the Future," *Medical Clinics of North America,* January, 1970.

On the reorganization of work, see O'Toole, *op. cit.* See also Robert L. Kahn, "The Work Module—A Tonic for Lunchpail Lassitude," *Psychology Today,* February, 1973.

The Free Self

Most of this chapter must remain without specific attributions. Anyone familiar with the writings of my father, Albert Edward Bailey, will find reflected stardust from the universe of his rich mind. See particularly "The Use of Art in Religious Education" (The Abington Press, 1922) and *Art and Character* (The Abington Press, 1938).

Harvey Cox has made a substantial contribution to my thinking about the free self. See particularly *The Feast of Fools* (Harper and Row, 1971).

My recent discovery of Joseph Campbell's beautiful work, *The Mythic Image* (Princeton University Press, 1975), added new perspectives to my inherited interest in art. Some of Lionel Trilling's writings have stretched my mind in delightful ways—especially *Sincerity and*

Authenticity: Six Lectures (Harvard University Press, 1971). George Leonard's *Education and Ecstasy* (Delacorte, 1968) at the school level, and Brand Blanshard, *The Uses of a Liberal Education, and Other Talks to Students* (Open Court, 1973), at the collegiate level, articulate existing and possible linkages between education and the free self. But once again, experience and reflection have been my most basic tutors.

As to specific references, note "TV at 25: The Intellectual in Videoland," *Saturday Review*, May 31, 1975, *passim.* Estelle Ramey's article, "Boredom: The Most Prevalent American Disease," is in *Harpers*, November, 1974. For a stunning analysis of the impact of TV upon the society, see Douglass Cater, *TV and the Thinking Person, A Policy Paper*, The Aspen Institute for Humanistic Studies, 1975, which, among other things, contains the reference to Michael Robinson. See also Douglass Cater and Stephen Strickland, *TV Violence and the Child* (Russell Sage, 1975), for a frightening story of TV-caused social pathology and the power of the telecommunications lobby.

A documentation on the drop in verbal and mathematical test scores is to be found in *College-Board Services 1974-75*, ATP, College Entrance Examination Board, 1975.

Homer's reference to the banquet and the harp is to be found in Edith Hamilton's exquisite study, *The Greek Way* (Norton, 1948), p. 34. Fortunately, in recent years there has been a heartening increase in cultural centers across the nation. See, "Upbeat for Music, Drama, Dance—New Growth of Cultural Centers," *U.S. News and World Report*, October 20, 1975, pp. 52-53.

Paul Fussell's *The Great War and Modern Memory* was published by Oxford University Press in 1975.

My reference to the mind being its own greatest frontier was prompted by, among other sources, the issue of the *Saturday Review* dedicated to "Inside the Brain: The Last Great Frontier," August 9, 1975.

See especially the opening essay by Albert Rosenfeld and Kenneth W. Klivington, pp. 13-15.

E. B. White, on the occasion of his 70th birthday, was interviewed by a *New York Times* reporter. See *New York Times,* July 11, 1969, pp. 1, 43.

The quotation from Harvey Cox is in *The Feast of Fools, op. cit.,* p. 13.

The Enveloping Polity

This chapter is the product of 25 years spent as a political scientist. My writings have been informed by a variety of experiences in practical politics at all levels of the American federal system. In the evolution of my own thought I have been particularly influenced by the writings of E. E. Schattschneider and Paul H. Appleby.

The quotation from Thucydides is taken from Hamilton, *The Greek Way, op. cit.,* pp. 187-188. The remaining quotations from traditional political theorists are taken from Sabine, *op. cit.* The statement by Edward Levi is to be found in an article by Warren Bennis, "Open Covenants Not So Openly Arrived At," *The Washington Post,* October 26, 1975, D2.

The Thurber aphorism was found in *Pageant,* April, 1961, p. 31. J. H. Elliott made his useful point in "The Mannerists," *Horizon,* summer, 1973. Incidentally, of all the journals I read, I find *Horizon* the most generally nourishing of the free self.

I am indebted to Roger W. Heyns for pointing out to me the contradiction between "negotiated settlements" and the "win/lose" value environment of contemporary America.

For a general survey of theoretical and historical models for training political leaders, see my article "Character Education for the Public Service," in Clarence H. Faust and Jessica Feingold (eds.), *Approaches to Education for Character: Strategies for Change in Higher Education* (Columbia University Press, 1969), pp. 137-151.

The quotation from T. Swann Harding is to be found in "The Marriage of Science to Government," *American Journal of Pharmacy,* October, 1944.

For an overview of traditional and emerging theories of education for public administration careers see the writings of Dwight Waldo, especially "Developments in Public Administration," *Annals,* Vol. 404, November, 1972, pp. 217-54; and "Education for Public Administration in the Seventies," in Frederick Mosher (ed.), *American Public Administration: Past, Present, and Future* (University of Alabama Press, 1976).

The final couplet is from Ralph Waldo Emerson's poem, "Boston," read in Faneuil Hall on December 16, 1873, on the Centennial Anniversary of the destruction of the tea in Boston Harbor, *Emerson's Works,* (G. Bell, 1914), p. 234.

Implications and Directions

Anyone interested in reforming the American educational system should begin by reading a sobering work by Ira S. Steinberg, *Educational Myths and Realities* (Addison-Wesley, 1968). Steinberg's basic stance is that ". . . schools are engaged permanently in the business of maintaining themselves in continued operation under the pressure of conflicting pushes and pulls without engendering or encouraging severe frictions in the community" (p. 237). In his colorful phrase, each school system is its own "individual swamp of accommodations" (p. 237). He contends that "Ambiguity is the glue that holds things together. It is the sponge that absorbs all." In consequence, Steinberg believes that we must give up the notion of educational decision making by synoptic overview (p. 240). He contends that general policy objectives may not, in fact, be easily translated into directives for technically feasible school practices: "to adopt school practices in the name of such objectives may be to promise to deliver what cannot be delivered thereby" (p. 228). I would submit that his general description of schools applies as well to most colleges and universities.

The issue for me, therefore, has been how to clarify some basic human needs that might be met in part by improved educational services without postulating a single, commanding pattern of educational reform. I am encouraged by the fact that many of the insights and propositions in my monograph stem from experiments recently or presently undertaken in this country. Fortunately, I am not writing in a vacuum. Others have sensed the same issues I have set forth, and are busily at work in their own settings attempting to put things right. This book is designed only to further encourage a process well under way. Another excellent reminder of the barriers facing those who would change education is to be found in John Goodlad, *The Dynamics of Educational Change* (McGraw-Hill, 1975).

Ralph W. Tyler comes close to being America's "Mr. Education." References in this chapter refer to "Educational Requirements for a Modern Democracy," *Center Report,* October, 1975, pp. 1-6.

School Administrative District #2 in Unity, Maine, has experimented with a four-day week/teachers center combination. For details, write to the State Education Department, Augusta, Maine. An excellent survey of the teachers center movement is to be found in Kathleen Devaney and Lorraine Thorne, *Exploring Teachers' Centers* (Far West Laboratory, 1975). See also my article, "Teachers' Centers: A British First," *Phi Delta Kappan,* November, 1971, pp. 146-149.

Many secondary schools in the mid-1970s are experimenting with work and community-service activities. See *25 Action Learning Schools,* National Association of Secondary School Principals, Reston, Virginia, 1975. See also, *Executive High School Interns of America Handbook,* Academy for Educational Development, 1975; and Richard Ferrin, Project Director, *Bridging the Gap: A Study of Education-to-Work Linkages,*

College Entrance Examination Board, June 18, 1975.

The reference to Wirtz is to *The Boundless Resource, op. cit.*

The directors of the four-day week program in Unity, Maine, conducted before-and-after tests that demonstrated gains for four-day week students in every basic skill except spelling where there was a marginal decline. How much of the gains were due to a "Hawthorne effect" is, of course, impossible to know.

Although I stand behind the generalization that few colleges and universities have addressed themselves to "the range of individual and societal needs that mark the existential realities of the last decade of the twentieth century," there are a number of heartening exceptions, some of which have been referred to in previous pages. The major national source of information about higher education innovation is NEXUS, an information retrieval system sponsored by the American Association for Higher Education. NEXUS' address and telephone number as of this writing are: 2000 P Street, N.W., Washington, D.C. 20036, (202) 785-8480. See also *Designing Diversity '75*, Conference Proceedings, 2nd National Conference on Open Learning and Nontraditional Study, June 17–19, Washington, D.C. (University of Mid-America, 1975).

The more responsible end of the Free University spectrum is addressing many of the issues raised in this book. See for example, *National Free University News*, No. 1, December, 1975, and *University for Man*, Manhattan, Kansas, Fall, 1975 bulletin of courses.

On the narrowing of the income gap between college-degree holders and nondegree holders, see Freeman and Hollomon, *op. cit.*

The Fund for the Improvement of Postsecondary Education, of the Department of Health, Education, and Welfare, has supported a number of experiments in educational brokering. See particularly James M. Heffernan, Francis U. Macy, and Donn F. Vickers, *Educational Brokering: A New Service for Adult*

Learners, Regional Learning Service of Central New York, November, 1975. See also Nancy Schlossberg and Alan D. Entine (eds.), "Coming of Age: Counseling Adults," *The Counseling Psychologist,* Vol. VI, No. 1, March, 1976.

Index